MW01069585

Second Edition

Strategic Reading 1

Jack C. Richards Samuela Eckstut-Didier

CAMBRIDGE UNIVERSITY PRESS
Cambridge, New York, Melbourne, Madrid, Cape Town,
Singapore, São Paulo, Delhi, Tokyo, Mexico City

Cambridge University Press
32 Avenue of the Americas, New York, NY 10013-2473, USA

www.cambridge.org
Information on this title: www.cambridge.org/9780521281126

First published 2012

Printed in Hong Kong, China, by Golden Cup Printing Company Limited

A catalog record for this publication is available from the British Library.

ISBN 978-0-521-28112-6 Student's Book
ISBN 978-0-521-28114-0 Teacher's Manual

Book design: TSI Graphics
Layout services: Page Designs International, Inc.
Photo research: TSI Graphics

Contents

Scope and Sequence

Unit	Readings	Reading Strategies
Unit 1 **Culture**	**1** Adventures in India **2** Body Language in the United States **3** Hot Spots in Cross-Cultural Communication	Making Inferences Predicting Previewing Vocabulary Recognizing Cause and Effect Skimming Thinking About the Topic Thinking About What You Know Thinking Beyond the Text Understanding Pronoun Reference
Unit 2 **Money**	**1** Shopaholics **2** Young Millionaires **3** Pity the Poor Lottery Winner	Identifying Main Ideas and Supporting Details Paraphrasing Previewing Vocabulary Recognizing Cause and Effect Skimming Understanding Pronoun Reference Understanding the Order of Events Thinking About the Topic
Unit 3 **Sports**	**1** The Ancient Olympic Games **2** The Greatest Marathon Runner **3** Extreme Sports	Predicting Previewing Vocabulary Recognizing Purpose Scanning Skimming Thinking About What You Know
Unit 4 **Music**	**1** Music and Moods **2** I'll Be Bach **3** The Biology of Music	Distinguishing Fact from Opinion Predicting Recognizing Cause and Effect Skimming Thinking About the Topic Understanding the Order of Events
Unit 5 **Animals**	**1** The Penguins of Brazil **2** Exotic Animals – Not as Pets! **3** Let's Abandon Zoos	Distinguishing Fact from Opinion Identifying Main Ideas and Supporting Details Making Inferences Previewing Vocabulary Recognizing Purpose Scanning Skimming Thinking About the Topic Thinking About What You Know
Unit 6 **Travel**	**1** Vacationing in Space **2** Ecotourism **3** Jet Lag	Predicting Previewing Vocabulary Recognizing Point of View Scanning Skimming Thinking About the Topic Understanding Cause and Effect Understanding Pronoun Reference

Unit	Readings	Reading Strategies
Unit 7 **The Internet**	**1** Love on the Internet **2** Help on the Internet **3** How Wikis Work	Predicting Recognizing Point of View Skimming Thinking About the Topic Thinking About What You Know Understanding the Order of Events
Unit 8 **Friends**	**1** Ten Easy Ways to Make Friends **2** Best Friends **3** Are Online Friends Real Friends?	Applying Information from the Text Identifying Main Ideas and Supporting Details Paraphrasing Predicting Previewing Vocabulary Scanning Skimming Thinking About the Topic
Unit 9 **Gifts**	**1** Gift Giving **2** Modern Day Self-Sacrifice **3** Gift Cards	Identifying Supporting Details Paraphrasing Predicting Recognizing Cause and Effect Skimming Thinking About the Topic Thinking About What You Know
Unit 10 **Emotions**	**1** Do You Have a Sense Of Humor? **2** Envy: Is It Hurting or Helping You? **3** The Value of Tears	Making Inferences Organizing Information into an Outline Predicting Recognizing Cause and Effect Skimming Thinking About the Topic Thinking About What You Know
Unit 11 **Food**	**1** Chocolate **2** Urban Farms **3** It Tastes Just Like Chicken	Identifying Supporting Details Predicting Previewing Vocabulary Recognizing Cause and Effect Recognizing Purpose Scanning Skimming Summarizing Thinking About What You Know
Unit 12 **Sleep and Dreams**	**1** Power Napping Is Good For the I.Q. **2** Common Questions About Dreams **3** What Is a Dream?	Predicting Scanning Skimming Summarizing Thinking About the Topic Thinking Beyond the Text Thinking About What You Know Understanding Pronoun Reference

Introduction

Overview

Strategic Reading is a three-level series for young adult and adult learners of English. As its title suggests, the series is designed to develop strategies for reading, vocabulary-building, and critical thinking skills. Each level features texts from a variety of authentic sources, including newspapers, magazines, books, and Web sites. The series encourages students to examine important topics in their lives as they build essential reading skills.

The first level in the series, *Strategic Reading 1*, is aimed at intermediate level students. It contains 12 units divided into three readings on popular themes such as sports, music, the Internet, and food. The readings in *Strategic Reading 1* range in length from 300 to 500 words and are accompanied by a full range of activities.

The units (and the readings within units) can either be taught in the order they appear or out of sequence. The readings and exercises, however, increase in difficulty throughout the book.

The Unit Structure

Each unit has the same ten-page structure. It includes a one-page unit preview and three readings, each of which is accompanied by two pre-reading tasks and four post-reading tasks.

Unit Preview

Each unit begins with a brief summary of the three readings in the unit. These summaries are followed by questions that stimulate students' interest in the readings and allow them to share their knowledge of the topic.

Pre-Reading Tasks

Each reading is accompanied by two pre-reading tasks: a reading preview task and a skimming or scanning task.

Reading Preview

Before each reading, students complete one of four types of pre-reading exercises: *Predicting, Previewing Vocabulary, Thinking About the Topic,* or *Thinking About What You Know*. These exercises prepare students to read and help them connect the topic of the reading to their own lives. Students identify information they expect to read, learn new vocabulary, write down what they know about the topic, or mark statements that are true about themselves.

Skimming/Scanning

One *Skimming* or *Scanning* exercise accompanies every reading. Before reading the whole text, students learn either to scan a text to look for specific information or to skim a text to get the gist. Other activities in this section ask students to confirm predictions from the reading preview section, compare their experiences with the writer's experiences, or identify the writer's opinion.

Post-Reading Tasks

Following each reading, are four post-reading tasks: A–D. These tasks respectively check students' comprehension, build their vocabulary, develop a reading strategy, and provide an opportunity for discussion.

A Comprehension Check

The task immediately following the reading is designed to check students' comprehension. In some cases, students check their understanding of the main ideas. In others, students have to delve more deeply into the text for more detailed information.

B Vocabulary Study

This section is designed to help students understand six to eight words that appear in the text. Students use contextual clues, recognize similarity in meaning between words, or categorize words according to meaning.

C Reading Strategy

An important part of *Strategic Reading* is reading strategy development. Students are introduced to a variety of strategies, such as making inferences, summarizing, and understanding pronoun reference. (For a full list of reading strategies see the Scope and Sequence on pages iv–v.) Practicing these strategies will help students gain a deeper understanding of the content of the text and develop the necessary strategies they will need to employ when they read on their own outside of the classroom. The section opens with a brief explanation of the reading strategy and why it is important.

D Relating Reading to Personal Experience

This section asks three open-ended questions that are closely connected to the topic of the reading. It gives students an opportunity to share their thoughts, opinions, and experiences in discussion or in writing. It is also a chance to review and use vocabulary introduced in the text.

Timed Reading

Each unit ends with an invitation for students to a timed reading task. Students are instructed to reread one of the texts in the unit, presumably the one they understand best, and to time themselves as they read. They then record their time in the chart on page 124 so that they can check their progress as they proceed through the book. (Naturally, there is no harm in students rereading and timing themselves on every text in a unit. However, this could be de-motivating for all but the most ambitious of students.)

Reading Strategies

Reading is a process that involves interaction between a reader and a text. A successful reader is a strategic reader who adjusts his or her approach to a text by considering questions such as the following:

- What is my purpose in reading this text? Am I reading it for pleasure? Am I reading it to keep up-to-date on current events? Will I need this information later (on a test, for example)?
- What kind of text is this? Is it an advertisement, a poem, a news article, or some other kind of text?
- What is the writer's purpose? Is it to persuade, to entertain, or to inform the reader?
- What kind of information do I expect to find in the text?
- What do I already know about texts of this kind? How are they usually organized?
- How should I read this text? Should I read it to find specific information, or should I look for the main ideas? Should I read it again carefully to focus on the details?
- What linguistic difficulties does the text pose? How can I deal with unfamiliar vocabulary, complex sentences, and lengthy sentences and paragraphs?
- What is my opinion about the content of the text?

Reading strategies are the decisions readers make in response to questions like these. They may prompt the reader to make predictions about the content and organization of a text based on background knowledge of the topic as well as familiarity with the text type. They may help the reader decide the rate at which to read the text – a quick skim for main ideas, a scan for specific information, a slower, closer reading for more detailed comprehension, or a rapid reading to build fluency. Other reading strategies help the reader make sense of the relationships among the ideas, such as cause and effect, contrast, and so on. In addition, the strategy of reading a text critically – reacting to it and formulating opinions about the content – is a crucial part of being a successful reader.

The *Strategic Reading* series develops fluency and confidence in reading by developing the student's repertoire of reading strategies. Students learn how to approach a text, how to choose appropriate strategies for reading a text, how to think critically about what they read, and how to deal with the difficulties that different kinds of texts may pose.

Jack C. Richards

Authors' Acknowledgments

We would like to thank Bernard Seal for his efforts in getting the project going, for his vision in setting the second edition down a new path, and for his insightful comments until the very end.

We are also grateful to the production and design staff that worked on this new edition of *Strategic Reading*: our in-house editors, Alan Kaplan, Brigit Dermott, and Chris Kachmar; TSI Graphics; and Don Williams, who did the composition.

For their useful comments and suggestions, many thanks to the reviewers: Laurie Blackburn, Cleveland High School, Seattle, Washington; Alain Gallie, Interactive College of Technology, Atlanta, Georgia; John Howrey, Nanzan University, Nagoya, Japan; Ana Morales de Leon, Instituto Tecnologico de Monterrey, Monterrey, Mexico; Sheryl Meyer, American Language Institute, University of Denver, Denver, Colorado; Donna Murphy-Tovalin, Lone Star College, Houston, Texas; Richard Patterson, King Saud University, Saudi Arabia; Byongchul Seo, Yonsei University, Seoul, South Korea.

Finally, a writer is nobody without a good editor. In that vein, we are grateful to Amy Cooper and Kathleen O'Reilly for their critical eye and their expert guidance. And to Amy Cooper in her role as project manager, we owe many thanks for her patience, understanding, and good sense of humor.

Jack C. Richards
Sydney, Australia

Sammi Eckstut
Melrose, Massachusetts, USA

UNIT 1

Culture

Look at the titles of the readings and their brief descriptions to preview this unit's content. Before you begin each reading, answer the questions about it.

Reading 1

Adventures in India

The writer of these journal entries shares her experiences as an exchange student in India, where she lived for one year.

1. Have you ever been to India? If so, what was the trip like? If not, is India a place you would like to visit? Why or why not?
2. How do you think life in your country is different from life in India? Explain your answer.
3. What would be good about living in a different country for a year? What would be difficult?

Reading 2

Body Language in the United States

How do people in the United States greet each other? What types of body language are common? In this excerpt from a book, you learn the answers.

1. How do people in your culture greet each other? Do they usually shake hands? Do they ever kiss or hug?
2. When people in your culture talk, how close to each other do they usually stand? Is it important for them to make eye contact?
3. Do you think body language in the United States is different from or similar to body language in other countries? Explain your answer.

Reading 3

Hot Spots in Cross-Cultural Communication

This article from the Internet discusses the differences in conversational styles around the world.

1. Is it easy to get along with people from different cultures? Why or why not?
2. Do you enjoy being with people from different cultures, or does it make you feel uncomfortable? Explain your answer.
3. In your culture, what topics do you usually talk about with people you don't know well? What topics would you avoid talking about?

Adventures in India

Thinking About the Topic

Imagine that you had to spend a year in a foreign country. How would you feel? Read the list of words from the reading. Look up any new words in a dictionary. Then check (✓) the words that describe how you might feel. Compare your answers with a partner.

_____ confused	_____ homesick	_____ ignorant	_____ lonely
_____ lost	_____ miserable	_____ scared	_____ tired

Skimming

Skim the reading to find out how the writer feels. Underline the words and phrases that describe her feelings. Then read the whole text.

1 I have spent a year in India on a student exchange program. These journal entries deal with the good and bad times that I went through there. They will give you an idea of what it is like to live in this country.

July 6

2 I suddenly have the feeling that I am alone in this unknown town. The stress of the last weeks has been gradually increasing, and I am feeling quite miserable. I met a Japanese student, and it is great to be able to share my feelings with somebody else. Of course, my Indian friends are very understanding. But if you're not a foreigner, you can't really understand how lonely a foreigner can feel.

August 5

We got on the train, slept, read, talked, ate, and watched the countryside. Before I realized what was happening, the 27 hours of travel were behind us. We had arrived in Delhi. 3

I really enjoyed that trip. We had almost a whole compartment to ourselves. I slept pretty well, even though it was noisy – I guess the train rocked me to sleep. The only problem was my painful stomachache. 4

September 9

A new group of students arrived today. They all look clean, fresh, and a little confused. They remind me of my arrival here. I suddenly realize how much I have learned and how much is more familiar to me now. I don't feel lost and ignorant anymore. I know how to find my way around town and how to use public transportation. It is quite a good feeling to be the one "who knows" – even though I don't know *that* much. 5

June 10

The last weeks have passed so quickly. I have only about a month left in this country. There's so much to do and so little time. My room is filled with things to pack, and my head is trying to summarize my "Indian experience." As the days go by, I try to think of all the things that I want to remember. My mind is full of small, daily, unimportant events that I couldn't have imagined a year ago. 6

June 23

The monsoon[1] seems to have started. During the last few weeks, it has rained from time to time. But the past couple of mornings, we have woken up to find our garden flooded. All this rain reminds me of my arrival here and how scared I felt then. 7

July 15

As my departure gets closer, I'm tired, and I look forward to going home. I want to see my country and family again – although I am sorry to leave India. I'm not homesick the way I was last winter. Now I wish I could take India back home with me. 8

---

[1] ***monsoon:*** the season of heavy rain in hot Asian countries

Adapted from www.climbtothestars.org/india/

A Comprehension Check

Match the date of the journal entry with its topic.

1. _____ July 6 — a. the weather
2. _____ August 5 — b. getting ready to leave
3. _____ September 9 — c. the train ride to Delhi
4. _____ June 10 — d. good and bad feelings about leaving India
5. _____ June 23 — e. better feelings about life in India
6. _____ July 15 — f. the need to meet people who understand you

B Vocabulary Study

Find the words and phrases in *italics* in the reading. Then circle the letters of the correct meanings.

1. *gradually* (par. 2)
   a. immediately
   b. slowly
2. *behind us* (par. 3)
   a. finished
   b. beginning
3. *even though* (par. 4)
   a. because
   b. although
4. *rocked* (par. 4)
   a. made a lot of noise
   b. moved from side to side
5. *familiar* (par. 5)
   a. not new anymore
   b. strange
6. *a month left* (par. 6)
   a. a month of experience
   b. a month before leaving

C Making Inferences

Sometimes the reader must infer, or figure out, what the writer did not explain or state directly in the text.

Make inferences about the writer's feelings about her trip. Were her feelings positive, negative, or both? Check (✓) the correct column.

The writer's feelings	Positive	Negative	Positive & negative
1. at the start of her stay in India		✓	
2. during the train ride to Delhi			
3. after about eight weeks in India			
4. about a month before she left India			
5. a few days before she left India			
6. about her year in India			

D Relating Reading to Personal Experience

Discuss these questions with your classmates.

1. Would you like to go to another country on a student exchange program? Why or why not?
2. If you could spend a year in another country, where would you go? Why? How do you think life there is different from life in your country?
3. What do you think exchange students usually find interesting or different about your country?

Body Language in the United States

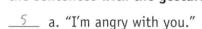

1

2

Thinking About What You Know

Look at the pictures. First tell your classmates which of these gestures are common in your culture and what they mean. Then think about what each gesture usually means in the United States. Work with a partner to match the sentences with the gestures.

3

4

5

__5__ a. "I'm angry with you."

____ b. "Hi. It's nice to see you."

____ c. "Good-bye."

____ d. "It's over there."

____ e. "Come here, please."

Skimming

Skim the reading to check your answers. Then read the whole text.

Here are some examples of body language that you might notice on a visit to the United States.

Greetings and good-byes

Most people shake hands and make eye contact when they meet people for the first time. Among very good friends, a woman may give another woman a little hug, and a man may kiss a woman quickly on the cheek. Males don't usually hug one another; however, this is changing. Men usually shake hands with the right hand. Sometimes they use the left hand to either cover the handshake or lightly hold the other person's arm. This shows greater warmth and friendship. 1

Most people wave hello or good-bye by extending the arm, palm facing outward, and twisting the hand at the wrist. Another way is to raise the arm, palm outward, and move the whole arm and hand back and forth. This is important to know because in many other countries, the same movements mean "no." 2

Body language in public

3 When people are waiting in a public place, such as the post office, they usually form lines. Some people get angry and complain if someone pushes their way into a line or jumps ahead of other people.

4 Many women still like men to open doors for them. They also like men to give up their seats on public transportation. However, some women do not like this type of behavior. They feel that men and women should be treated in the same way.

5 There are two common ways to ask someone to come over to you: Sometimes, people raise an index finger and then bend and straighten it quickly. Other times, they raise a hand (palm facing inward) and curl the fingers quickly towards themselves. Either way is polite. To call a waiter, people generally just raise one index finger to head level or above.

6 It is common and polite for people to use the hand and index finger to point at objects or to show directions.

Body language in business and social life

7 People in the United States usually stand about one arm's length away from each other while talking or standing together. This space is called "the comfort zone."

8 In the United States, it's important to make direct eye contact in business and social situations. If you don't make eye contact, people will probably think that you are bored or not interested.

9 If there is silence in these situations, people usually try to make conversation. Periods of silence make many people uncomfortable.

Body language with children

10 In the United States, mothers sometimes show that they are angry with children by shaking an index finger at them. People may show that they like children by patting them on the top of the head.

Adapted from *Gestures: The Do's and Taboos of Body Language Around the World*

A Comprehension Check

Mark the statements about body language in the United States *T* (true) or *F* (false). Then correct the false statements. The first one is marked for you.

__F__ 1. When men shake hands, they use the ~~right~~ left hand to cover the handshake.

_____ 2. A woman might greet a friend with a little hug or a kiss.

_____ 3. It's common for women with babies to push ahead in a line of people.

_____ 4. Some women don't want men to give up their seats on pubic transportation.

_____ 5. It's not polite for people to use the hand and index finger to show directions.

_____ 6. People do not usually make eye contact with each other during a business meeting.

_____ 7. During a conversation, a long period of silence is unusual.

_____ 8. An angry mother sometimes shakes an index finger at her young child.

B Vocabulary Study

Find the words in *italics* in the reading. Then match the words with their meanings.

____ 1. *wave* (par. 2)	a. move a part of the body so that it isn't straight
____ 2. *extend* (par. 2)	b. move the hand or arm from side to side
____ 3. *twist* (par. 2)	c. touch lightly
____ 4. *jump* (par. 3)	d. move suddenly
____ 5. *bend* (par. 5)	e. change the position of a body part by turning it
____ 6. *pat* (par. 10)	f. stretch

C Thinking Beyond the Text

Good readers are able to go beyond the words that a writer actually uses and understand ideas that are never directly expressed. One way to practice this strategy is to imagine other information that the writer could have added about the topic.

Read the statements in the chart. If these statements were added to the reading, which section would they each fit into? Check (✓) the correct heading.

	Greetings and good-byes	Body language in public	Body language in business and social life	Body language with children
1. Parents may also put an index finger in front of their lips to signal "Be quiet."				
2. They even hold the door open for men sometimes.				
3. However, you should never point at other people.				
4. Males don't usually kiss each other, either.				
5. You should also never look down at your feet when you talk at a meeting.				

D Relating Reading to Personal Experience

Discuss these questions with your classmates.

1. Which information in the reading is true in your culture? Which information is not true?
2. What are three things that foreign visitors should know about polite and impolite body language in your culture?
3. If you saw visitors using impolite body language, would you correct them? Why or why not?

Reading 3

Hot Spots in Cross-Cultural Communication

Predicting

Read the title and the section headings of the reading. (*Hot spots* are places where there is trouble.) Then check (✓) the information that you think you will read about. Compare your answers with a partner.

_____ 1. different conversational styles

_____ 2. differences in body language

_____ 3. ways of ending conversations

_____ 4. how loudly or softly people speak

_____ 5. the importance of silence

_____ 6. the subjects that people talk about

Skimming

Skim the reading to find which topics are and are not in the reading. Then read the whole text.

1 In today's business world, we often meet people from cultures that are different from our own. These differences can lead to misunderstandings. For successful communication, it's important to know some ways that conversational styles may differ around the world.

2 **Opening and closing conversations:** Different cultures have different ways of greeting people. They also have rules about who speaks first and how a conversation starts and ends. For example, when North Americans end a conversation, they often say, "We must get together again soon." However, this is usually just a form of politeness and not a real invitation.

3 **Taking turns during conversations:** In some cultures, people take turns during a conversation. In other cultures, it's more polite to listen quietly until someone asks you to speak. This is especially true when one person is older than the other or in a more senior position in a company.

Interrupting: In some parts of the world, people often interrupt each other and express 4
strong opinions. To Northern Europeans and North Americans, this kind of conversation may sound like an argument, but it is not. It's just a different conversational style.

Use of silence: In North America, if there is silence for more than twenty seconds 5
during a meeting, people become uncomfortable. They usually break the silence by talking. However, this doesn't happen everywhere. In some places, a period of silence after someone has spoken shows respect for the speaker.

Appropriate topics of conversation: Topics of conversation also differ around the 6
world. In some places, people don't talk about their families with strangers. Most North Americans, however, think family life is a good topic. In addition, people in some cultures feel free to ask questions about how much something costs or how much someone earns. For North Americans, money issues are private and inappropriate for conversation with people they don't know well.

Use of humor: North Americans often use humor to "break the ice," or make others 7
feel comfortable. However, in some cultures, people think laughing and humor show disrespect. They never use humor with strangers.

Knowing how much to say: In some cultures, people usually take time to make a point 8
in a discussion. They might start with a long introduction to their point and end with a long conclusion. North Americans often speak more directly. This may seem impolite to people who are not used to it.

Timing: When is it appropriate to introduce a sensitive topic into a conversation? 9
Consider, for example, two business people who have a disagreement about money. In some cultures, it would be more polite to discuss less sensitive topics first. In other cultures, it would be fine to talk about the disagreement early in the conversation. For successful cross-cultural communication, it's very important to talk about the right thing at the right time.

Adapted from http://www.SchulerSolutions.com

A Comprehension Check

Read the statements about conversational styles. Where is each statement true? Check (✓) the correct column.

	In North America	In some other parts of the world
1. It's unusual to interrupt a lot during a conversation.		
2. Periods of silence show respect.		
3. People often talk about their family with someone they don't know well.		
4. People often talk about money with someone they don't know well.		
5. It's common to use humor with strangers.		
6. People take a long time before they talk about a serious topic.		

B Vocabulary Study

Write the opposites of the words in italics. Add one of these prefixes that means "not": *dis-*, *im-*, *in-*, *mis-*, or *un-*. Look back at the reading to find the correct forms.

1. Good friends have an *understanding* of each other's thoughts and feelings. But even good friends sometimes say things that cause misunderstandings. (par. 1)
2. In a North American classroom, it is usually *appropriate* to raise your hand before answering a question. It is ______________ to just shout out the answer. (par. 6)
3. When you treat people nicely because you admire them, you show *respect*. When you do not treat people nicely, you show ______________. (par. 7)
4. It is *polite* to say "please" and "thank you." A person who does not use these words is ______________. (par. 8)
5. When you have an *agreement* with someone, you feel *comfortable*. When you have a ______________, you probably feel stressed and ______________. (par. 9 & 5)

C Understanding Pronoun Reference

Writers use different kinds of pronouns to refer to information that is stated earlier in a text. Some common pronouns are *it*, *this*, and *they*. Understanding pronoun reference is very important for reading comprehension.

What do the pronouns in italics refer to? Circle the letter of the correct answer.

1. *They* (par. 2, line 2)
   a. different cultures
   b. different ways
2. *this* (par. 2, line 5)
   a. a conversation
   b. "We must get together again soon."
3. *This* (par. 3, line 6)
   a. take turns talking
   b. listen quietly until someone asks you to speak
4. *it* (par. 4, line 3)
   a. this kind of conversation
   b. an argument
5. *This* (par. 8, line 3)
   a. start with a long introduction
   b. speak more directly

D Relating Reading to Personal Experience

Discuss these questions with your classmates.

1. What are some features of conversational style in your culture?
2. In what ways is conversational style in your culture similar to North American conversational style? In what ways is it different?
3. Why do you think it's important for people to understand the differences in conversational styles around the world?

Reread one of the unit readings and time yourself. Note your reading speed in the chart on page 124.

UNIT 2

Money

Look at the titles of the readings and their brief descriptions to preview this unit's content. Before you begin each reading, answer the questions about it.

Reading 1

Shopaholics

For some people, shopping can become a problem. Read this article to learn why and to find out how these people can get help.

1. How often do you go shopping? Where do you shop? At malls? On the Internet?
2. Why do people go shopping? Is it always because they need something?
3. Do you know people who buy things that they can't afford? Explain your answer.

Reading 2

Young Millionaires

How do some people become millionaires at a young age? What skills and ideas do they have? This article has some answers.

1. Would you like to be a millionaire? Why or why not?
2. Do you think it's possible for a person to have a multimillion dollar business before the age of 20? Why or why not?
3. Who are some famous millionaires? How did they become wealthy?

Reading 3

Pity the Poor Lottery Winner

This magazine article explains why winning the lottery is not always a good thing.

1. Do you ever play the lottery? If so, have you ever won anything?
2. How do you think your life would change if you won the lottery?
3. What could be some unpleasant results of winning the lottery?

Shopaholics

Previewing Vocabulary

The words in the box are from the reading. Discuss the meanings of the words with a partner. Look up any new words in a dictionary. Then write each word in the correct column.

advertisements	boredom	consumer	depression
financial	guilt	loneliness	price tags
purchases	shame	shopping bags	stress

Words related to shopping	Other words

Skimming

Skim the reading to find out how the words in the "Other words" column above are related to shopaholics. Then read the whole text.

1 TV. The Internet. The mall. Everywhere we look, we see advertisements that urge us to buy, buy, buy. In today's consumer society, we are under constant pressure to shop. Of course, most people only buy what they need and what they can afford. However, there are some people, called shopaholics, who cannot control their desire to spend money and

buy things. This kind of addictive behavior can lead to overwhelming financial problems, family conflict, and deep unhappiness.

What are the symptoms of a shopaholic? People with this problem often spend hours and hours shopping on the Internet or at the mall. Their closets are full of clothing and jewelry that they have never worn, with the price tags still on them. Their homes may be packed with shopping bags and boxes that overflow with things that they bought but never used: kitchen gadgets, books, electronics, DVDs, and dozens of other items. Many shopaholics are aware of their problem, but when they go to a store, they simply cannot resist the urge to buy. Some of them are ashamed of their weakness and try to hide it by storing their purchases in places like the attic, where others won't see them. 2

Psychologists suggest there are several reasons for a shopping addiction. For some people, it is a way of relieving stress. For others, shopping is a way to fight loneliness or depression. For people with low self-esteem, shopping can be a way that they prove their self-worth. Sometimes the problem develops out of boredom. It becomes a replacement for other hobbies and interests, and it helps pass the time. Although shopping can temporarily make people feel good, they often experience feelings of shame and guilt later. 3

When shopping habits get out of control, people need professional help. They can either see a counselor or join an organization such as Shopaholics Anonymous. Groups like this try to help people understand the reasons for their addiction and learn how to control the urge to shop. Their goal is to help people find ways to fulfill themselves that do not lead to serious debt and troubled lives. 4

A Comprehension Check

Circle the letter of the best main idea for each paragraph.

1. Paragraph 1
   a. People shop a lot at malls and on the Internet.
   b. People who are shopaholics have a shopping problem.
   c. Shopaholics can have family problems.

2. Paragraph 2
   a. There are several symptoms of a shopaholic.
   b. Shopaholics buy things that they do not need.
   c. Shopaholics do not want others to see their purchases, so they often hide them in the attic.

3. Paragraph 3
   a. Shopaholics often have too much stress.
   b. Some shopaholics feel loneliness or depression.
   c. There are different reasons why people become shopaholics.

4. Paragraph 4
   a. Some people's shopping habits are out of control.
   b. There is professional help available for shopaholics who need it.
   c. Professional organizations try to help shopaholics understand why they shop.

B Vocabulary Study

Find the words in *italics* in the reading. Then match the words with their meanings.

_____ 1. *overwhelming* (par. 1)	a. something that a person cannot stop doing
_____ 2. *addiction* (par. 3)	b. money that someone owes
_____ 3. *self-esteem* (par. 3)	c. a person who gives advice
_____ 4. *counselor* (par. 4)	d. very great
_____ 5. *urge* (par. 4)	e. a strong need or desire
_____ 6. *debt* (par. 4)	f. the opinion that people have of themselves

C Recognizing Cause and Effect

When you read, it is important to recognize the reason why something happens (the cause). It is also important to recognize what happens as a result (the effect).

Use the information in the reading to decide whether each statement is a cause of shopping or an effect of shopping. Write *C* (cause) or *E* (effect).

__C__ 1. You need a new pair of shoes.

_____ 2. You are bored.

_____ 3. You are in debt.

_____ 4. You have clothes in your closet that you never wear.

_____ 5. You hide purchases from your family.

_____ 6. You see an advertisement.

_____ 7. You have an urge to go out and spend money.

_____ 8. You need professional help.

D Relating Reading to Personal Experience

Discuss these questions with your classmates.

1. Do you know anyone who might be a shopaholic? What are his or her symptoms?
2. What advice would you give to a friend who is a shopaholic?
3. Do you and others in your community feel the constant pressure to shop and buy new things? If so, why, and what do you do about it?

Young Millionaires

Previewing Vocabulary

The words and phrases in the box are from the reading. Discuss their meanings with a partner. Look up any new words in a dictionary. Compare your answers with a partner.

characteristics in common	creativity	have vision
the Internet	late teens	passionate
self confidence	set goals	take risks

Scanning

Scan the reading to find and circle the words and phrases. Discuss how you think they relate to the topic of the reading. Then read the whole text.

Today's millionaires are younger than ever. Many are in their late teens or early twenties. They are people like Mark Zuckerberg, who started the popular social networking site Facebook before he turned 20. Another example is Michael Dell. Dell started a company that sells computers directly to customers at cheaper prices than stores can offer. He was a millionaire by age 19. And Jermaine Griggs became a millionaire by the time he was 23. Griggs developed a very successful Web site that helps people learn to play the piano, guitar, or drums. So what does it take for a young person to become a millionaire?

2 Young millionaires have several characteristics in common. They are smart, they have vision, and they have a lot of determination. They set goals for themselves and put a lot of time and effort into finding ways to achieve them. They have self-confidence and work hard to persuade other people that they have a good idea. They are more likely to take risks because they usually don't have family responsibilities yet.

3 These young people also develop good business skills. They research what it takes to run a business well. They study the lives of successful business people. They also use the Internet to test out new ideas and to get instant feedback on what works and what doesn't.

4 Success in business depends on finding solutions to problems or satisfying a particular need. It also depends on marketing something in a creative way so that people will want it. This takes creativity, another important characteristic of young millionaires.

5 Consider these other examples of young people who profited from their creative business ideas:

- Catherine Cook realized that teenagers needed their own social networking site. She and her two brothers started myYearbook, especially for teens. Cook became a millionaire before she was 20.
- Sean Belnick was fascinated by businesses that sell things on the Internet. He started an online business selling office chairs, and became a millionaire at 16.
- Chris Mittelstaedt started a business delivering fresh fruit to workplaces in his twenties. To advertise the delivery service, Mittlestaedt dressed up in a banana costume, and he got a lot of attention. A few years later, he had a multi-million dollar business.

6 None of these successful young people started out with the goal of becoming a millionaire. They all had a business idea that they were passionate about. They were determined to make their vision a reality. They didn't give up when they ran into difficulties. And they really believed in themselves.

A Comprehension Check

Complete the chart with information about the young millionaires in the reading.

Young millionaire	Age when the person started the business or became rich	Type of business
1. Mark Zuckerberg	before he turned 20	
2. Michael Dell		
3. Jermaine Griggs		
4. Catherine Cook		
5. Sean Belnick		
6. Chris Mittelstaedt		

B Vocabulary Study

Find the words and phrases in the box in the reading. Then complete the sentences.

determination (par. 2)	achieve (par. 2)	run (par. 3)
profited (par. 5)	ran into (par. 6)	give up (par. 6)

1. At first, we ________________ a lot of problems, but we solved all of them.
2. If you can't hit the ball at first, don't ________________. You'll improve your skills with practice.
3. She hopes to ________________ great success in her new business.
4. He ________________ greatly from the useful advice that his friends gave him.
5. She will ________________ her father's company after he retires next year.
6. He studied hard because of his ________________ to do well on the final exam.

C Identifying Main Ideas and Supporting Details

Identifying the main ideas and supporting details in a text is an important strategy that will help your reading comprehension. It's a good idea to find the main ideas first. Then look for the supporting details that explain the main ideas more fully.

In each pair of statements, decide which is the main idea and which is the supporting detail. Mark each statement *MI* (main idea) or *SD* (supporting detail).

1. ____ a. Today's millionaires are younger than ever.
   ____ b. They are people like Mark Zuckerberg, who started the popular social networking site Facebook before he turned 20.
2. ____ a. They are smart, they have vision, and they have a lot of determination.
   ____ b. Young millionaires have several characteristics in common.
3. ____ a. They research what it takes to run a business well.
   ____ b. These young people also develop good business skills.
4. ____ a. Success in business depends on finding solutions to problems or satisfying a particular need.
   ____ b. Catherine Cook realized that teens needed their own social networking site.

D Relating Reading to Personal Experience

Discuss these questions with your classmates.

1. What characteristics do you have in common with young millionaires?
2. What problems do you think people may have if they become rich and successful at a very young age?
3. What is a new product or new idea that you think could make a lot of money?

Pity the Poor Lottery Winner

Thinking About the Topic

Check (✓) the statements that you think are true. Then discuss your answers with a partner.

_____ 1. Lottery winners sometimes have trouble with their friends and family.

_____ 2. Suddenly winning a lot of money does not always bring you happiness.

_____ 3. Most happy lottery winners are religious, with strong family ties.

_____ 4. People shouldn't spend money on the lottery.

_____ 5. People try to kidnap lottery winners.

Skimming

Skim the reading to find which statement above is the main idea. Then read the whole text.

NEW JERSEY LOTTERY
TRENTON, NJ
April 30, 2002
Pay to the order of
Jorge & Joanne Lopes
$ 58.9 Million
Dollars
Fifty-eight million-nine-hundred thousand
Acting Executive Director
Treasurer of the United States.

Most of us think that if we won millions in a lottery, it would solve all our problems. 1
In fact, winning the lottery often brings big trouble. Take the case of Cindy, who won a $2.5 million prize. As with many winners, at first she was excited. She soon got a shock, however, when her friend said, "What right did you have to win?" Cindy hardly ever bought lottery tickets. However, her friend always bought tickets, and she really needed money. She was supposed to go with Cindy to buy those tickets, but at the last minute, her plans changed, and she couldn't go. When Cindy won the lottery, her friend felt cheated. Other unpleasant surprises came from her family. Her mother thought Cindy ought to share the prize money with her sister. When Cindy disagreed, she and her mother didn't speak to each other for six years.

William "Bud" Post won $16.2 million in the lottery, but he was broke five years later. 2
Even worse, his brother was in jail. He had hired someone to murder Bud and his wife so that he could get the money for himself. Post said he was happier before he won the lottery, when all he had was a job with a circus. After he won, his friends and family either begged him for money or borrowed it from him all the time.

Of course, sometimes there are happy winners. They tend to have close family ties, 3
strong religious faith, and a firm sense of who they are. When Lydia Neufeld won $17 million, she and her husband, Dave, bought a church for their community, and Dave gave his business to his employees.

However, most lottery winners have problems. Consider Paul McNabb, a baker who 4
became Maryland's first lottery millionaire. He received kidnap threats about his children, thieves broke into his house, and he had to give up his job. Worst of all, he lost his trust in other people. In spite of all this, McNabb said he wouldn't want to give the money back. He was enjoying it. But would he do it again? "No way," he laughed.

Adapted from *The New York Times Magazine*

A Comprehension Check

Who had these experiences? Complete the statements with *Cindy*, *William*, or *Paul*.

1. ______________ was broke five years after winning the lottery.
2. ______________ had a friend who felt cheated.
3. ______________ didn't trust people anymore.
4. ______________'s children were in danger.
5. ______________ didn't talk to a family member for years.
6. ______________ had a family member who would kill to get the money
7. ______________ had friends who were always asking for money.

B Vocabulary Study

Find the words in *italics* in the reading. Then circle the letters of the correct meanings.

1. *shock* (par. 1)	a. a big surprise	b. a medical condition
2. *broke* (par. 2)	a. damaged	b. having no money
3. *hired* (par. 2)	a. asked for work	b. paid someone to work for you
4. *tend* (par. 3)	a. want	b. be likely
5. *faith* (par. 3)	a. friends	b. belief in something
6. *broke into* (par. 4)	a. robbed	b. divided

C Paraphrasing

Paraphrasing means using your own words to say what you have read. This is one strategy that you can use to improve your understanding of a text.

Circle the letter of the best paraphrase for each sentence from the reading.

1. *Pity the poor lottery winner.* (title)
   a. Feel bad for the winner of the lottery.
   b. Imagine being the winner of the lottery.
2. *What right did you have to win?* (par. 1)
   a. How did you win?
   b. Why did you win?
3. *When Cindy won the lottery, her friend felt cheated.* (par. 1)
   a. After Cindy's success, her friend felt that some of the prize money belonged to her.
   b. Her friend felt that Cindy had won the lottery dishonestly.
4. *William "Bud" Post won the lottery, but he was broke five years later.* (par. 2)
   a. Bud was poor for five years and then he won the lottery.
   b. Bud was poor five years after he won the lottery.

D Relating Reading to Personal Experience

Discuss these questions with your classmates.

1. Do you think Cindy's friend was wrong to feel cheated? Why or why not?
2. If you won money, would you share it with anyone? If so, with whom? Why?
3. If you won money, how would you spend it?

Reread one of the unit readings and time yourself. Note your reading speed in the chart on page 124.

UNIT 3

Sports

Look at the titles of the readings and their brief descriptions to preview this unit's content. Before you begin each reading, answer the questions about it.

Reading 1

The Ancient Olympic Games

Who could compete in the ancient Olympics? What were the prizes? Find the answers to these questions and many more in this article.

1. Do you enjoy watching the Olympic Games? Why or why not? What are your favorite Olympic sports?
2. What sports do you think were in the ancient Olympic Games that are also in the modern Olympics?
3. Do you like to see the greatest athletes win? Or do you always want the athletes from your country to win? Explain your answer.

Reading 2

The Greatest Marathon Runner

Many different kinds of people compete in marathons. Read about one special competitor who ran in the Boston Marathon.

1. Do you enjoy running? Why or why not?
2. Have you ever seen a marathon? What do you know about marathons?
3. What skills are required for success in running a long-distance race?

Reading 3

Extreme Sports

This reading describes some of the most popular extreme sports today.

1. Which sports do you participate in? Which sports do you like to watch?
2. Do you like sports that require you to take risks? Why or why not?
3. What are some examples of dangerous, risky sports? Why do you think people participate in these sports?

The Ancient Olympic Games

Thinking About the Topic

How much do you know about the ancient Olympic Games? Mark each statement *T* (true) or *F* (false). Compare your answers with a partner.

_____ 1. Only men and boys could compete in the ancient Olympics.

_____ 2. Only married women could attend the ancient Olympics.

_____ 3. The winners of the ancient Olympics got a crown made of leaves from an olive tree.

_____ 4. The judges of the ancient Olympics came from many different parts of the Greek Empire.

_____ 5. The penalty for cheating in the ancient Olympics was death.

Skimming

Skim the reading to check your answers. Then read the whole text.

1 Today the Olympic Games are the world's largest show of athletic skill and competitive spirit. This was also true of the ancient Olympic Games. They were part of a major religious festival honoring Zeus, the most important Greek god. People from all the different parts of the Greek world came to the games to watch and take part. Sometimes, like today, these people were political rivals.

Who could compete in the Olympics?

2 The Olympics were open to any freeborn Greek.[1] There were separate men's and boys' divisions for the events. The judges divided athletes into the boys' or men's divisions according to physical size, strength, and age.

[1] ***freeborn Greek:*** a Greek person who was not a slave

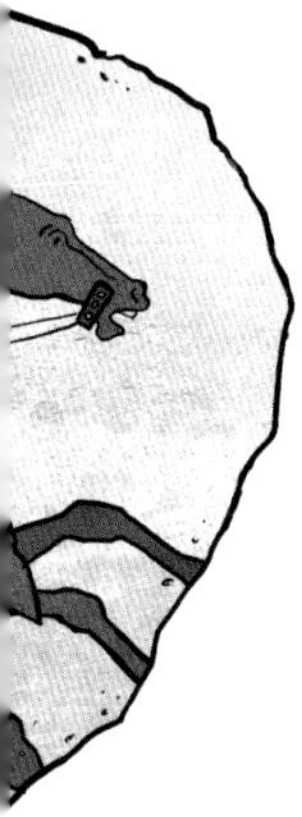

Women were not allowed to compete in the Games. However, they could enter 3
equestrian events as the owner of a chariot team or an individual horse and participate that way.

Were women allowed at the Olympics?

Unmarried women were allowed to attend the games, but they were forbidden to 4
participate in any physical competition. Married women were not even permitted to attend the games, under penalty of death.

What prizes did the Olympic winners get?

The winners did not get money prizes, but each one received a crown made from olive 5
leaves. He could also have a statue of himself set up in Olympia, the site of the Olympic Games. An athlete's success increased the fame and reputation of his community in the Greek world. Therefore, when a winner returned home, people treated him as a celebrity. It was common for winners to eat all their meals at public expense. They also had front-row seats at the theater and other public festivals. One city even built a private gym for its Olympic wrestling champion to exercise in.

Who were the Olympic judges?

Unlike the modern Olympics, judges of the ancient Games did not come from all over 6
the world. They were Eleans, that is, from Elis, a local region that included Olympia.

Even though the judges were all from Elis, Elians were allowed to compete in the 7
Olympics because they had a reputation for fairness. Other Greeks believed that Eleans would never cheat at the Games.

What was the penalty for cheating?

The judges fined anyone who violated the rules. The money was used to build statues 8
of Zeus on the road to the stadium in Olympia.

Adapted from www.perseus.tufts.edu/Olympics/faq1.html

A Comprehension Check

Read these facts about the modern Olympics. For each fact about the modern Olympics, discuss with a partner how the ancient Olympics were different.

1. Nationalism, money, and politics are part of the modern Olympics.
2. Women compete in a lot of different events in the modern Olympics.
3. Women can attend all the events in the modern Olympics.
4. Winners in the modern Olympics receive medals as prizes.
5. Judges in the modern Olympics come from all over the world.
6. Anyone who cheats in the modern Olympics has to leave the Games.

B Vocabulary Study

Find the noun forms of the words in column A in the reading. Write the nouns in column B. Then match the nouns in column B with their meanings in column C.

A	B		C
1. *divide* **v.**	divisions	(par. 2)	a. following the rules
2. *athletic* **adj.**	______________	(par. 2)	b. the cost of something
3. *strong* **adj.**	______________	(par. 2)	c. separations
4. *famous* **adj.**	______________	(par. 5)	d. people who are skilled in a sport
5. *expensive* **adj.**	______________	(par. 5)	e. physical power
6. *fair* **adj.**	______________	(par. 7)	f. the state of being very well-known

C Understanding Pronoun Reference

Writers use different kinds of pronouns to refer to information that is stated earlier in a text. Some common pronouns are *they, one, its*. Understanding pronoun reference is very important for reading comprehension.

What do the pronouns in *italics* refer to? Circle the letter of the correct answer.

1. *They* (par. 1, line 2)	a. the Olympic Games	b. the ancient Olympic Games
2. *they* (par. 3, line 1)	a. Women	b. Games
3. *one* (par. 5, line 1)	a. winner	b. prize
4. *They* (par. 5, line 5)	a. winners	b. meals
5. *its* (par. 5, line 7)	a. city	b. gym

D Relating Reading to Personal Experience

Discuss these questions with your classmates.

1. What do you think ancient Greeks would find most surprising about the modern Olympic Games?
2. Would you like to have the Olympics in your hometown? Why or why not?
3. Is it important for the Olympic Games to continue? Why or why not?

The Greatest Marathon Runner

Predicting

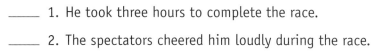

You are going to read about a man who took part in a marathon while on crutches.[1] Check the statements that you think describe what happened. Compare your answers with a partner.

_____ 1. He took three hours to complete the race.

_____ 2. The spectators cheered him loudly during the race.

_____ 3. Some runners were angry that he was in the race.

_____ 4. He kept stopping to rest during the race.

_____ 5. He ran part of the race on one leg.

[1] ***crutches:*** supports made of wood, metal, or plastic that help people walk if they do not have legs or if they have problems with their legs

Skimming

Skim the reading to see which statements you predicted correctly. Then read the whole text.

The Boston Marathon is the oldest annual race in the world. This long-distance running event began in 1897. Like all marathons, the distance is 26.2 miles (about 42 kilometers). To enter, you must first qualify, and about 20,000 athletes qualify each year. Within that number are some who are known as "mobility impaired."[2] They might be in wheelchairs or have an artificial leg or arm. They start the marathon two hours before the other runners. 1

[2] ***mobility impaired:*** not having or not being able to move some parts of the body

2 I will never forget the first time that I ran in the Boston Marathon. A truly amazing thing happened when I was halfway through the race. Ahead of me, there was a man who had only one leg. He was using a pair of crutches to help him run. Every runner who ran past him called out some words of praise and encouragement.

3 I finished my race that day in just under 3 hours and 30 minutes. After finding my family, we went back to our hotel room, and I shared the story of the runner with one leg. I wanted my children to know how special he was. He was competing in a world-famous event. For him, this was a far greater accomplishment than for runners like me. I wanted my children to understand what that meant.

4 After resting a bit, at around 6 p.m. we decided to go watch the last of the runners pass the finish line. By this time, there were only a few runners left in the race. As we stood there, I began to hear people cheering. The cheers grew louder and more powerful. Then I saw the man on crutches getting closer and closer to the finish. It was 8 hours and 15 minutes after the mobility-impaired runners had started. As he approached the end, he suddenly raised his crutches up in the air and completed the last stretch on one leg. To watch him pass the finish line was the most amazing and inspiring experience of my life, one that my children and I still talk about.

5 I have a personal motto that I try to live and train by. "There is no great goal achieved without greater sacrifice." To me it means that the journey toward your goals is often more difficult than actually reaching the goal itself. And people who make that journey, like the runner that day, inspire those around them.

Adapted from http://www.faithfulsoles.com/StoriesAll/00001-TheGreatestMarathoner.htm

A Comprehension Check

Circle the letter of the correct answer.

1. What do we know about the writer?
   a. He ran the Boston Marathon more than one time.
   b. He has run in different marathons around the world.
   c. He hopes to be a great marathon runner in the future.

2. Why were the people cheering at the finish line?
   a. They wanted the race to end.
   b. They wanted the man with one leg to win.
   c. They thought the man with one leg was amazing.

3. Why did the writer think the man with one leg was the "greatest marathon runner"?
   a. He won the marathon.
   b. He did something that was very difficult.
   c. He didn't use his crutches at the end of the race.

4. Why did the man with one leg not use his crutches at the end of the race?
   a. He didn't need the crutches anymore.
   b. The crutches were bothering him and making him go more slowly.
   c. He wanted to prove to himself that he could do something difficult.

B Vocabulary Study

Find the words and phrases in *italics* in the reading. Then circle the correct meanings.

1. An *annual* event happens **every year** / **every 10 years**. (par. 1)
2. Something that is *artificial* is **real** / **not real**. (par. 1)
3. When he *called out* to the runner, he **shouted** / **talked on the phone**. (par. 2)
4. When she *approached* the finish line, she went **away from** / **near** it. (par. 4)
5. A *motto* is a sentence that shows something a person **believes** / **wants**. (par. 5)
6. When you make a *sacrifice*, you give up something so that you can have something else that is **less** / **more** important. (par. 5)
7. If people *inspire* you, they give you **confidence and the desire** / **good luck and the ability** to do something. (par. 5)

C Understanding the Order of Events

Understanding the order of events in a text means that you know what happens first, second, third, and so on. This information helps you understand the ideas in the text.

Number the sentences from *1* (first event) to *9* (last event). The first one is marked for you.

_____ a. The writer rested.

_____ b. The writer started the race.

_____ c. The writer finished the race.

_____ d. The writer returned to the finish line.

_____ e. The runner with one leg started the race.

_____ f. The runner with one leg finished the race.

_____ g. The writer passed the runner with the one leg.

_____ h. The runner with one leg stopped using his crutches.

__*1*__ i. The writer and the runner with one leg qualified.

D Relating Reading to Personal Experience

Discuss these questions with your classmates.

1. Would you like to run in a marathon? Why or why not?
2. The writer says his motto is "There is no great goal achieved without greater sacrifice." Do you agree or disagree? What examples can you give?
3. Is there someone who has inspired you in your life? Explain your answer.

Reading 3

Extreme Sports

1

2

3

4

5

6

Previewing Vocabulary

The words and phrases in the box are from the reading. Discuss their meanings with a partner. Look up any new words in a dictionary. Then next to each word or phrase below, write the number of a related picture. For some pictures, more than one number is possible.

_____ crest of a wave	_____ elastic cord	_____ gears	_____ glider
_____ handlebars	_____ hiking	_____ snowboard	_____ steep, rocky cliffs

Scanning

Scan the reading to find and circle the words and phrases in the box. Then read the whole text.

1 Extreme sports give people a strong sense of risk, thrill, and excitement. They are physically demanding, and they often involve speed and height. One reason many people participate in extreme sports is because of the "adrenaline rush"[1] they get. Another reason is because they like a challenge. People who choose extreme sports want to experience something very different from daily life.

2 Even though they may be dangerous, extreme sports are popular with people in many parts of the world. Some people like to participate in these sports, while others just like to watch them. Here are some of the most popular extreme sports.

---

[1] ***adrenaline rush:*** a sudden, intense feeling of excitement that the adrenal gland produces when the body is under stress

Bungee jumping: This sport involves jumping from a very tall structure, such as a bridge or 3 high building, while attached to a long elastic cord. The excitement comes from the free fall after you jump. The cord stops you at the end of the fall and makes you bounce up and down. Bungee jumping was first done in New Zealand but is now common in many countries.

Hang gliding: In this air sport, you pilot a hang glider, a very light aircraft that does not have a 4 motor. Most people only use the movements of their bodies to control the glider. Hang gliders can fly very high and cover great distances and can also perform amazing stunts in the sky.

Mountaineering: This is one of the most popular sports. It combines mountain hiking and 5 climbing. Sometimes it includes skiing in snow-covered areas. Maybe this sport is so popular because it can be more extreme or less extreme depending on the difficulty of the mountain you choose to climb. It is a sport that any physically fit person can do.

Mountain biking: Mountain bikes have stronger frames than other bikes. They are usually 6 wider and have larger tires. The gears are designed to help bikers climb steep hills and ride over rough areas. The handlebars allow you to sit up straighter than on other bikes. Mountain biking activities include riding over rough, open areas in the country and riding up and down steep hills. Some mountain bikers do stunts while riding.

Surfing: A surfer rides the crest of a wave as it rolls toward the shore. The most extreme 7 surfers ride huge waves that are more than 20 feet (about 6 meters) high. There are two different types of surfboards: long and short. Each type of board requires a different surfing style. Surfing is probably one of the oldest extreme sports. It has been part of Polynesian culture for hundreds of years, but today it is popular around the world.

Snowboarding: Snowboarding began with a man's gift for his daughter. He tied two skis 8 together. There was a rope in the front for her to steer with. Standing on this snowboard, his daughter could "surf" downhill in the snow. This toy, the Snurfer (from the words *snow* and *surf*) became hugely popular. Over time, people improved the original design, leading to the modern snowboard. Today, expert snowboarders try death-defying tricks and turns on their boards. They challenge themselves by snowboarding in mountainous places with deep snow and obstacles such as steep, rocky cliffs.

A Comprehension Check

Write the name of the sport that matches each description.

1. This sport is popular in the winter: ____________________
2. This is one of the oldest extreme sports: ____________________
3. People who don't like too much risk can do this: ____________________
4. You can't be afraid of heights to do these sports: ____________________ and ____________________
5. You spend time in the sky when you do this sport: ____________________
6. You do these sports where the land is steep: ____________________, ____________________, and ____________________

B Vocabulary Study

Match the words from the reading that are similar in meaning.

____ 1. *very* (par. 1)	a. *challenge* (par. 1)
____ 2. *dangerous* (par. 2)	b. *stunts* (par. 6)
____ 3. *cord* (par. 3)	c. *rope* (par. 8)
____ 4. *control* (par. 4)	d. *steer* (par. 8)
____ 5. *difficulty* (par. 5)	e. *hugely* (par. 8)
____ 6. *tricks* (par. 8)	f. *death-defying* (par. 8)

C Recognizing Purpose

Writers create texts for different purposes. For example, sometimes a writer wants to teach readers how to do something. Sometimes a writer wants to influence the reader's thinking in some way. Other times a writer wants to give information. Recognizing a writer's purpose will help you better understand what you read.

Check (✓) the writer's main purpose in the reading. Discuss the reasons for your answer with a partner.

____ 1. to teach people how to do different extreme sports

____ 2. to warn people about the dangers of different extreme sports

____ 3. to give general information about different extreme sports

____ 4. to convince people to try different extreme sports

D Relating Reading to Personal Experience

Discuss these questions with your classmates.

1. Which of the extreme sports mentioned in the article would you like to try? Which ones would you never try? Why?
2. Can you think of a person you know or a famous athlete who does extreme sports? Which sport does this person do? Why do you think he or she likes extreme sports?
3. Where is the nearest place for you to go if you want to participate in or just watch the extreme sports mentioned in the article?

Reread one of the unit readings and time yourself. Note your reading speed in the chart on page 124.

UNIT 4

Music

Look at the titles of the readings and their brief descriptions to preview this unit's content. Before you begin each reading, answer the questions about it.

Reading 1

Music and Moods

Feeling sad? Why not change your mood with music? This magazine article explains the effect of music on your emotions.

1. How often do you listen to music? What kinds of music do you listen to?
2. What kind of music makes you happy? What kind makes you sad?
3. Do you ever listen to music when you are in a bad mood? Does it help you?

Reading 2

I'll Be Bach

Today composers can use computer technology to compose music. In this article from the Internet, you learn about the experiences of a modern-day classical music composer.

1. Do you listen to classical music? Why or why not?
2. Who is your favorite composer? Why do you like his or her music?
3. Do you think you could recognize music that was composed by a computer? Why or why not?

Reading 3

The Biology of Music

This magazine article discusses the connections among music, communication, and the human brain.

1. In what ways do humans use music to communicate with each other?
2. Does music usually have a strong effect on your emotions? Explain your answer.
3. Which of the following can you do: sing in tune, play a musical instrument, remember the notes of a piece of music, or recognize music that you've heard before?

Music and Moods

Thinking About the Topic

When do you listen to certain kinds of music? Match the phrases in the columns to make true sentences about you. You can use the letters more than once. Compare your answers with a partner.

	When . . .	I listen to . . .
______	1. I want to cheer up,	a. music with a fast tempo.
______	2. I want to relax,	b. music with lots of percussion, such as drums.
______	3. I want to have energy,	c. music with string instruments, such as violins.
		d. music with a slow tempo.
		e. music with a strong beat, such as Latin music.

Skimming

Skim the reading to find the connections that the writer makes between music and moods.

Have you ever felt a sudden feeling of joy because you heard a favorite song playing? Then you know that music can have a strong effect on your emotions. Try to take advantage of this power of music. It can help get you out of a bad mood or stay in a good mood, says Alicia Ann Clair, professor of music therapy at the University of Kansas. Music can also help you relax and feel rejuvenated. 1

To cheer up or boost your energy, listen to Latin music or anything with a strong beat, lots of percussion, and a fast tempo. When you want to relax after a busy day, music with string instruments and woodwinds, less percussion, and a slower tempo can calm you. 2

Listen to calming music before you start any stressful activities, advises Dr. Clair. "Once you're in a good state of mind, it's easier to maintain it." You can lower stress at work with music, too, by playing relaxing tunes. But only play them when you really need them. "If you listen to them all day long, you'll stop noticing them." Dr. Clair explains. Then the music won't have any effect. 3

You can change your mood by switching from one kind of music to another. To feel rejuvenated, "Start with something serene and relaxing, and then gradually increase the tempo and beat," says Dr. Clair. For example, first play some nice gentle ballads, and then listen to something more energetic. When you want to calm down after a busy week at work, just do the opposite. 4

Adapted from *Woman's Day*

A Comprehension Check

Every paragraph in the reading has one main idea. Write the correct paragraph number for each main idea.

_____ a. This paragraph tells you how to change your mood with music.

_____ b. This paragraph describes music that can change your level of energy.

_____ c. This paragraph explains why music is an important part of your life.

_____ d. This paragraph describes music that can help you with stress.

B Vocabulary Study

Find the words and phrases in *italics* in the reading. Then circle the correct meanings.

1. When you feel *rejuvenated*, you feel **sleepy** / **energetic**. (par. 1 & 4)
2. When you *boost* something, you have **more** / **less** of it. (par. 2)
3. When you are in *a good state of mind*, you are **feeling fine**/ **thinking a lot**. (par. 3)
4. When you change your mood by *switching* music, you do so by **listening to** / **changing** it. (par. 4)
5. *Serene* music is **loud and fast** / **peaceful and calm**. (par. 4)
6. A *ballad* is a **slow love song** / **fast dance song**. (par. 4)

C Recognizing Cause and Effect

When you read, it is important to recognize the reason why something happens (the cause). It is also important to recognize what happens as a result (the effect).

Match each cause to its effect according to the reading.

CAUSE	EFFECT
_____ 1. Your favorite song comes on the radio.	a. You have more control over your mood.
_____ 2. You play some relaxing music.	b. Your energy level is increasing.
_____ 3. You're listening to Latin music.	c. You suddenly feel happy.
_____ 4. You understand the power of music.	d. The music doesn't change your mood at all.
_____ 5. You listen to calm music all day.	e. The way you feel changes.
_____ 6. You play a ballad and then some fast dance music.	f. You feel less stress.

D Relating Reading to Personal Experience

Discuss these questions with your classmates.

1. What is your favorite piece of music or song? Why is it your favorite?
2. What is your favorite musical instrument? Why do you like it?
3. What is a good piece of music or a song to listen to before you do something stressful?

J.S. Bach

I'll Be Bach

Predicting

The words in the box are from the reading. Discuss the meanings of the words with a partner. Look up any new words in a dictionary. Then look at the picture and the reading title and answer the questions below with your partner.

brains	compositions	computer program	database
melodies	opera	patterns	software

1. Who was J.S. Bach? Who do you think David Cope is?
2. How are Bach and Cope similar? How are they different?

Skimming

Skim the reading to check your answers. Then read the whole text.

Composer David Cope is the inventor of a computer program that writes original works of classical music. It took Cope 30 years to develop the software. Now most people can't tell the difference between music by the famous German composer J.S. Bach (1685–1750) and the Bach-like compositions from Cope's computer. 1

It all started in 1980 in the United States, when Cope was trying to write an opera. He was having trouble thinking of new melodies, so he wrote a computer program to create the melodies. At first this music was not easy to listen to. What did Cope do? He began to rethink how human beings compose music. He realized that composers' brains work like big databases. First, they take in all the music that they have ever heard. Then they take out the music that they dislike. Finally, they make new music from what is left. According to Cope, only the great composers are able to create the database accurately, remember it, and form new musical patterns from it. 2

3 Cope built a huge database of existing music. He began with hundreds of works by Bach. The software analyzed the data: It broke it down into smaller pieces and looked for patterns. It then combined the pieces into new patterns. Before long, the program could compose short Bach-like works. They weren't very good, but it was a start.

4 Cope knew he had more work to do – he had a whole opera to write. He continued to improve the software. Soon it could analyze more complex music. He also added many other composers, including his own work, to the database.

5 A few years later, Cope's computer program, called "Emmy," was ready to help him with his opera. The process required a lot of collaboration between the composer and Emmy. Cope listened to the computer's musical ideas and used the ones that he liked. With Emmy, the opera took only two weeks to finish. It was called *Cradle Falling*, and it was a great success! Cope received some of the best reviews of his career, but no one knew exactly how he had composed the work.

6 Since that first opera, Emmy has written thousands of compositions. Cope still gives Emmy feedback on what he likes and doesn't like of her music, but she is doing most of the hard work of composing these days!

David Cope and his computer, Emmy

Adapted from http://www.slate.com/id/2254232

A Comprehension Check

Circle the letter of the correct answer.

1. What kind of music does David Cope compose?
   a. classical music
   b. many different kinds of music
2. What was Cope's goal?
   a. He wanted to study Bach's music.
   b. He wanted to write an opera.
3. What did Cope realize about a composer's brain?
   a. It works like a big database.
   b. It can create melodies.
4. Who is Emmy?
   a. a composer who helped David Cope
   b. a computer program
5. Who wrote the opera *Cradle Falling*?
   a. David Cope
   b. David Cope and a computer program

B Vocabulary Study

Find the words in *italics* in the reading. Then match the words with their meanings.

_____ 1. *original* (par. 1)

_____ 2. *analyze* (par. 4)

_____ 3. *complex* (par. 4)

_____ 4. *collaboration* (par. 5)

_____ 5. *reviews* (par. 5)

_____ 6. *feedback* (par. 6)

a. information that tells you how well or badly you're doing something

b. reports that give opinions about music, books, or plays

c. not a copy

d. study something in a careful way

e. having many parts

f. the act of working together

C Understanding the Order of Events

> **Understanding the order of events in a text means that you know what happens first, second, third, and so on. This information helps you understand the ideas in the text.**

Number the events in the order they happened, from *1* (first) to *8* (last). The first one is marked for you.

_____ a. The computer software analyzed the database and created new patterns of music.

_____ b. He wrote a computer program to create the melodies for him.

_____ c. The computer program helped Cope write a successful opera.

_____ d. Cope built a huge database of existing music.

_____ e. He had trouble thinking of new melodies for the opera.

_____ f. Cope kept improving the software.

__*1*__ g. David Cope wanted to write an opera.

_____ h. The program didn't write very good music.

D Relating Reading to Personal Experience

Discuss these questions with your classmates.

1. Would you like to try composing music? Would you use computer software? Why or why not?
2. If you wanted to compose music with a computer, what music would you choose for the database?
3. Do you think that, in 100 years' time, people will still be writing music, or will computers do all the composing? Explain your answer.

The Biology of Music

Thinking About the Topic

Check (✓) the statements about music that you agree with. Compare your answers with a partner.

_____ 1. You have to be a musician to communicate through music.

_____ 2. Music has a magical effect on our feelings.

_____ 3. People with brain injuries can't make or listen to music.

_____ 4. Music can help you find a mate, that is, a husband or wife.

_____ 5. Making music requires good health.

Skimming

Skim the reading to find which of the statements the writer agrees with.

1 Humans use music as a powerful way to communicate. It may also play an important role in love. But what is music, and how does it work its magic? Science does not yet have all the answers.

2 What are two things that make humans different from animals? One is language, and the other is music. It is true that some animals can sing (and many birds sing better than a lot of people). However, the songs of animals, such as birds and whales, are very limited. It is also true that humans, not animals, have developed musical instruments.

3 Music is strange stuff. It is clearly different from language. However, people can use music to communicate things – especially their emotions. When music is combined with speech in a song, it is a very powerful form of communication. But, biologically speaking, what is music?

If music is truly different from speech, then we should process music and language in different parts of the brain. The scientific evidence suggests that this is true. 4

Sometimes people who suffer brain damage lose their ability to process language. However, they don't automatically lose their musical abilities. For example, Vissarion Shebalin, a Russian composer, had a stroke in 1953. It injured the left side of his brain. He could no longer speak or understand speech. He could, however, still compose music until his death ten years later. On the other hand, sometimes strokes cause people to lose their musical ability, but they can still speak and understand speech. This shows that the brain processes music and language separately. 5

By studying the physical effects of music on the body, scientists have also learned a lot about how music influences the emotions. But why does music have such a strong effect on us? That is a harder question to answer. Geoffrey Miller, a researcher at University College, London, thinks that music and love have a strong connection. Music requires special talent, practice, and physical ability. That's why it may be a way of showing your fitness to be someone's mate. For example, singing in tune or playing a musical instrument requires fine muscular control. You also need a good memory to remember the notes. And playing or singing those notes correctly suggests that your hearing is in excellent condition. Finally, when a man sings to the woman he loves (or vice versa[1]), it may be a way of showing off. 6

However, Miller's theory still doesn't explain why certain combinations of sounds influence our emotions so deeply. For scientists, this is clearly an area that needs further research. 7

---

[1] ***vice versa:*** a phrase used to show that the opposite of a situation is also true

Adapted from *The Economist*

A Comprehension Check

Mark each statement *T* (true) or *F* (false). Then correct the false statements. The first one is marked for you.

__F__ 1. Humans, ~~but not~~ and animals, can sing.

_____ 2. People can use music to communicate their emotions.

_____ 3. We use the same part of the brain for music and language.

_____ 4. Shebalin couldn't compose music after his stroke.

_____ 5. Geoffrey Miller has done research on music and emotions.

_____ 6. You need good muscle control to remember musical notes.

_____ 7. Memory is not an important part of making music.

_____ 8. Science does not know all the answers about the effects of music on humans.

B Vocabulary Study

Find the words in the box in the reading. Then complete the sentences.

limited (par. 2)	evidence (par. 4)	automatically (par. 5)
processes (par. 5)	fitness (par. 6)	showing off (par. 6)

1. Fred is dancing in front of a lot of women. He's ________________ again.
2. She can only play two pieces on the piano. Her ability is ________________.
3. When you see a red traffic light, you should ________________ stop your car.
4. Today scientists know a lot about how the brain ________________ language.
5. He's good with children. This shows his ________________ to be a good father.
6. Whales use song to communicate with each other. Scientists have a lot of ________________ that proves it.

C Distinguishing Fact from Opinion

When you read a text, it is important to be able to tell the difference between facts (information that is known to be true) and opinions (ideas that are based on the writer's feelings or beliefs).

Mark each statement *F* (fact) or *O* (opinion).

__O__ 1. It [music] may play an important role in love. (par. 1)

____ 2. It is true that some animals can sing. (par. 2)

____ 3. Music is strange stuff. (par. 3)

____ 4. It [music] is clearly different from language. (par. 3)

____ 5. Vissarion Shebalin could no longer speak or understand speech. (par. 5)

____ 6. When a man sings to the woman he loves, it may be a way of showing off. (par. 6)

D Relating Reading to Personal Experience

Discuss these questions with your classmates.

1. When birds sing, what do you think they are communicating? What about whales?
2. What other emotions besides love can music communicate?
3. Which is a more powerful form of communication for you, speech or music? Explain your answer.

Reread one of the unit readings and time yourself. Note your reading speed in the chart on page 124.

UNIT 5

Animals

Look at the titles of the readings and their brief descriptions to preview this unit's content. Before you begin each reading, answer the questions about it.

Reading 1

The Penguins of Brazil

In this newspaper article, the writer describes his unusual experience with a penguin.

1. Have you ever seen a penguin? If so, where did you see it? What do you remember about the experience?
2. Have you ever seen a wild animal when you didn't expect to? Where was it? What happened?
3. What can happen to an animal when it leaves its natural habitat, or natural home?

Reading 2

Exotic Animals – Not As Pets!

Imagine having a wild animal as a pet. This newspaper article discusses some of the problems.

1. Why do people like to have pets?
2. What kinds of animals do people in your country like to have as pets?
3. Which of these animals do you think make good pets: dogs, cats, turtles, rabbits, mountain lions, snakes, leopards, alligators, monkeys, parrots?

Reading 3

Let's Abandon Zoos

Is it right or wrong to capture, cage, and display animals in zoos? This letter to the editor of a newspaper expresses one opinion.

1. What is the purpose of a zoo?
2. When was the last time you went to the zoo? What zoo did you visit?
3. What do you like about zoos? What don't you like?

The Penguins of Brazil

Thinking About What You Know

How much do you know about penguins? Check (✓) the statements that are correct. Compare your answers with a partner.

_____ 1. Penguins can **flap** their wings.

_____ 2. Penguins eat small fish like **anchovies**.

_____ 3. Penguins swim in the **ocean**.

_____ 4. Penguins like to spend a lot of time on **hot sand**.

_____ 5. Penguins live in the **southern parts of South America**.

_____ 6. Penguins like warmer waters better than **colder waters**.

Scanning

Scan the reading to find the words and phrases in bold above. Check your answers. Then read the whole text.

1 It was a perfect summer morning on the beach in Rio de Janeiro. A man set up his umbrella and chair near the water. There was hardly anyone else around, and he was looking forward to reading his book. Just then, when he looked toward the sea, he noticed a small shape that emerged from the water. It slowly made its way out onto the sand and began to flap its wings. It was obviously very feeble and tired.

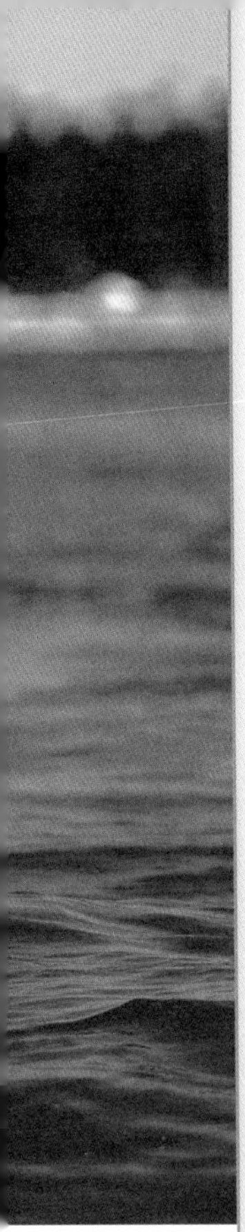

2 When the creature was just a few feet away, the man couldn't believe his eyes. A penguin? On a beach in Rio? Penguins don't belong in Rio. The man was amazed. He looked around to see if there was anyone else nearby to witness this strange sight.

3 A jogger soon appeared, followed by another. They stopped and stared. It was clear that the penguin was having trouble breathing. The first jogger looked at the sea and said, "Poor fellow, so far away from home."

4 The penguin fell to its side. It had swum 2,000 miles, trying to find the tiny anchovies that penguins like to eat. Why did the penguin need to travel so far? Perhaps it was confused by shifting ocean currents and temperatures – common effects of global warming.[1] The penguin needed help. It would not survive on the hot sand.

5 One of the joggers phoned for help, and soon some firemen arrived. The man was relieved that the penguin would soon be safe, although he felt a little sad, too. That weak, helpless creature suddenly made him understand the impact of humans on the planet.

6 The event on the beach at Rio happened some time ago. It was only the beginning of penguin migration to Brazil. Since that time, hundreds of penguins have appeared on the coasts of Brazil. They come all the way from Patagonia and the Straits of Magellan, southern parts of South America. They land on the sands exhausted and starving. People often rush to help them, but they don't know what to do, and many of the penguins die. Some are shipped or flown back to colder waters farther south.

7 Perhaps the experience of the penguins will help us better understand the serious effect of human activity on climate change and on the condition of our planet.

[1] ***global warming:*** a gradual increase in the earth's temperature caused by gases, especially carbon dioxide, that surround the earth

Adapted from http://www.nytimes.com/2009/11/29/opinion/29ribeiro.html?ref=penguins

A Comprehension Check

Circle the letter of the correct answer.

1. Why did the man go to the beach?
   a. He wanted to see a penguin.
   b. He wanted to relax.
2. Why were the people at the beach surprised?
   a. The penguin was far away from home.
   b. The penguin was having trouble breathing.
3. Why did the penguin travel so far from its home?
   a. It was looking for food.
   b. There were anchovies in the water near the beach in Rio.
4. Was this the only time a penguin appeared on the Brazilian coast?
   a. No, it was the first of many times that it happened.
   b. No, it was the last of many times that it happened.
5. Why was the man a little sad?
   a. He was never going to see the penguin again.
   b. He was thinking about the bad effects of human activity on Earth.

B Vocabulary Study

Match the words and phrases from the reading that are similar in meaning.

____ 1. *small* (par. 1)	a. *emerged* (par. 1)
____ 2. *made its way out* (par. 1)	b. *was amazed* (par. 2)
____ 3. *feeble* (par. 1)	c. *looked* (par. 3)
____ 4. *tired* (par. 1)	d. *tiny* (par. 4)
____ 5. *couldn't believe his eyes* (par. 2)	e. *weak* (par. 5)
____ 6. *stared* (par. 3)	f. *exhausted* (par. 6)
____ 7. *impact* (par. 5)	g. *effect* (par. 7)

C Recognizing Purpose

Writers create texts for different purposes. For example, sometimes a writer wants to give information. Sometimes a writer wants to influence the reader's thinking in some way. Other times a writer wants to entertain the reader with a story. Recognizing a writer's purpose will help you better understand what you read.

Check (✓) the writer's main purpose in the reading. Discuss the reasons for your answer with a partner.

____ 1. to tell the reader an enjoyable story

____ 2. to give information about penguins

____ 3. to describe what people are doing about global warming

____ 4. to make people think about the effect of global warming on the planet

D Relating Reading to Personal Experience

Discuss these questions with your classmates.

1. Have you ever observed an animal in its natural habitat? If so, what kind of animal was it? What was it doing?
2. What other effects can global warming have on animal life?
3. What are some ways that people are helping animals in danger to survive?

Exotic Animals — Not As Pets!

Thinking About the Topic

Exotic animals are not good pets. Check (✓) the reasons why you think this is true. Compare your answers with a partner.

_____ 1. Wild animals can be dangerous.

_____ 2. Wild animals can make people ill.

_____ 3. Wild animals are not happy in small spaces.

_____ 4. It costs a lot of money to feed wild animals.

_____ 5. Wild animals may behave badly in a home.

Skimming

Skim the reading to find out what the writer's reasons are. Then read the whole text.

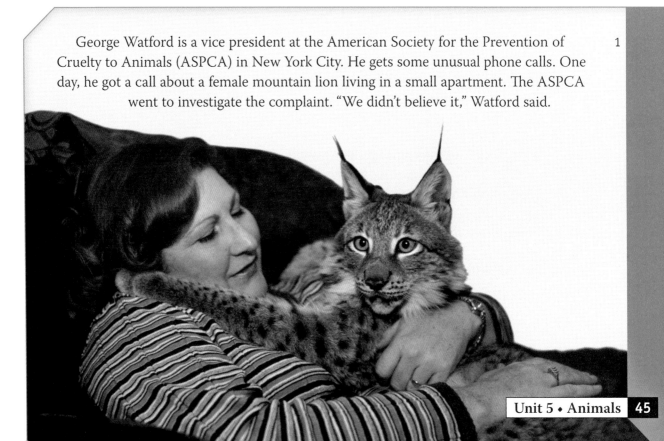

George Watford is a vice president at the American Society for the Prevention of Cruelty to Animals (ASPCA) in New York City. He gets some unusual phone calls. One day, he got a call about a female mountain lion living in a small apartment. The ASPCA went to investigate the complaint. "We didn't believe it," Watford said. 1

"But when we went out there, sure enough, there's a mountain lion sitting at the front window looking out at us." The big cat's owner knew that his neighbors were unhappy about the animal. He didn't try to stop ASPCA officials who removed it and took it to an animal preserve.

2 If you think that cramped city apartments are a poor habitat for wild animals, you are right. That still doesn't stop some people from keeping just about any type of animal that can fit inside their home. In one year, the ASPCA's city shelters took in 9,459 different animals, not counting cats and dogs. That number includes a lot of rabbits and turtles, but the ASPCA has also taken alligators, a leopard, and many other exotic pets from people's homes. These animals can't be released into the wild because they wouldn't survive. The ASPCA tries to find homes for them in zoos or animal preserves.

3 It's illegal to sell wild animals or poisonous snakes in New York City. Many apartment buildings don't even allow dogs and cats, not to mention more exotic animals. Still, the ASPCA takes away most of the exotic animals not because of complaints, but because the pet's owner needs help. A cute lion or bear cub will eventually grow up to be a dangerous predator. "When they bite, it isn't because they hate you today. It's because they're wild animals," said exotic animal expert Kathi Travers. She has the bite marks and scars to prove it.

4 Travers is quick to lecture against raising wild animals as pets. Too often people think that caring for a wild animal is the same as caring for a parrot or a poodle. "To love an animal is not enough," Travers said. "There has to be respect, and respect is not taking a squirrel monkey, sticking it in a little cage, and expecting the animal to be happy."

Adapted from *Newsday*

A Comprehension Check

Mark each statement *T* (true) or *F* (false). Then correct the false statements. The first one is marked for you.

F 1. City apartments are ~~good~~ poor places for wild animals.

____ 2. The ASPCA is an organization in the United States.

____ 3. Some cities have laws against selling wild animals.

____ 4. When animals bite, it's because they are exotic.

____ 5. Animals have bitten Kathi Travers.

____ 6. The ASPCA finds homes for exotic animals in the wild.

B Vocabulary Study

Find the words in the reading that match these definitions.

1. land kept in its natural state for wild animals ___preserve___ (par. 1)
2. not having enough space ________ (par. 2)
3. given freedom ________ (par. 2)
4. continue to live ________ (par. 2)
5. a baby lion or bear ________ (par. 3)
6. an animal that hunts, kills, and eats other animals ________ (par. 3)

C Identifying Main Ideas and Supporting Details

Identifying the main ideas and supporting details in a text is an important strategy that will help your reading comprehension. It's a good idea to find the main ideas first. Then look for the supporting details that explain the main ideas more fully.

In each pair of statements, decide which is the main idea and which is the supporting detail. Mark each statement *MI* (main idea) or *SD* (supporting detail).

1. ____ a. George Watford got a phone call about a mountain lion living in a small apartment.

   ____ b. The ASPCA gets some unusual calls.

2. ____ a. There is a variety of wild animals in people's homes.

   ____ b. The ASPCA has taken away alligators, a leopard, and other exotic pets from people.

3. ____ a. You shouldn't keep a wild animal as a pet.

   ____ b. A cute lion or bear cub will eventually grow up to be a dangerous predator.

4. ____ a. A wild animal is not the same as a pet.

   ____ b. Squirrel monkeys will not be happy in a little cage.

D Relating Reading to Personal Experience

Discuss these questions with your classmates.

1. Why do you think some people want an exotic animal such as a mountain lion, a snake, or a monkey as a pet?
2. What are some other possible problems with wild animals that the article did not discuss?
3. What are some things that people can do if they are no longer able to take care of a pet?

Let's Abandon Zoos

Previewing Vocabulary

The words in the chart are from the reading about zoos. Discuss the meanings of the words with a partner. Look up any new words. Then decide if each word has a positive or negative meaning.

	Positive	Negative
1. unnatural		
2. fair		
3. decent		
4. protective		
5. bored		
6. lonely		
7. abnormal		
8. self-destructive		

Scanning

Scan the reading to find and circle words from the chart that the writer uses to describe animals in zoos. Then read the whole text.

To the editor:

I would like to share my thoughts in response to your recent articles about zoos.

1 When did we lose our compassion for living creatures? How could we display animals in cages in unnatural environments – mostly for our entertainment? How could we possibly think that this was fair and decent treatment?

Zoo officials say that they are concerned about animals. However, most zoos remain 2
"collections" of interesting "items" rather than protective habitats. Zoos teach people that it is acceptable to keep animals in captivity. However, animals in zoos are bored, cramped, lonely, and far from their natural homes.

Zoos claim to educate people, but in fact, visitors don't learn anything meaningful 3
about the natural behavior, intelligence, or beauty of animals. Most zoo enclosures are quite small, and visitors can rarely observe animals' normal behavior in these unnatural spaces. Nor can they learn much from the labels on cages, which list only the species' name, diet, and where it normally lives.

The animals are kept together in small spaces, with no privacy and little opportunity 4
for mental stimulation or physical exercise. This results in abnormal and self-destructive behavior called zoochosis. In a worldwide study of zoos, the Born Free foundation found that zoochosis is common among animals in small spaces or cages. Another study found that elephants spend 22 percent of their time engaging in abnormal behaviors, such as repeated head movements or biting cage bars. Bears spend 30 percent of their time walking back and forth. These are all signs of distress.

Zoos also claim to save animals from extinction. However, zoos that breed endangered 5
animals, such as big cats and Asian elephants, often do not release them to the wild. Zoos talk a lot about their breeding programs. One reason is to ease people's worry about endangered species. The other reason is to attract a lot of customers who enjoy seeing baby animals. How many contests have we seen to name baby animals?

Ultimately we will save endangered species only if we save their habitats. We also need 6
to stop people from killing them. Instead of supporting zoos, we should support groups that work to protect animals and preserve their homes in the wild.

Adapted from *The Buffalo News*

A Comprehension Check

Check (✓) the statements that the writer probably agrees with.

_____ 1. Zoo officials care more about entertaining people than they care about the animals.

_____ 2. Animals in zoos are not happy.

_____ 3. Visitors to zoos learn a lot of important information about the animals.

_____ 4. Animals in zoos have problems that animals in the wild do not have.

_____ 5. Breeding programs in zoos do not save animals from extinction.

_____ 6. We should build better zoos to help animals.

B Vocabulary Study

Find the words and phrases in *italics* in the reading. Then circle the letters of the correct meanings.

1. *abandon* (title)
   a. continue using
   b. stop using
2. *compassion* (par. 1)
   a. a great love of beautiful things
   b. a feeling of sadness for the problems of others
3. *captivity* (par. 2)
   a. a place where animals can go where they want
   b. a place where animals are not free
4. *mental stimulation* (par. 4)
   a. something that encourages brain activity
   b. something that encourages sleeping
5. *distress* (par. 4)
   a. interesting behavior
   b. great suffering
6. *breeding* (par. 5)
   a. adult animals having baby animals
   b. baby animals living in zoos

C Distinguishing Fact from Opinion

When you read a text, it is important to be able to tell the difference between facts (information that is known to be true) and opinions (ideas that are based on the writer's feelings or beliefs).

Mark each statement *F* (fact) or *O* (opinion).

__O__ 1. When did we lose our compassion for living creatures? (par. 1)

____ 2. Zoos teach people that it is acceptable to keep animals in captivity. (par. 2)

____ 3. Most zoo enclosures are quite small, . . . (par. 3)

____ 4. . . . zoochosis is common among animals in small spaces or cages. (par. 4)

____ 5. Bears spend 30 percent of their time walking back and forth. (par. 4)

____ 6. Ultimately, we will save endangered species only if we save their habitats. (par. 6)

D Relating Reading to Personal Experience

Discuss these questions with your classmates.

1. Do all zoos treat animals the same way? Explain your answer. Give examples if possible.
2. What suggestions do you have to make zoos better for animals?
3. Do you agree with the writer of the letter? Why or why not?

Reread one of the unit readings and time yourself. Note your reading speed in the chart on page 124.

UNIT 6

Travel

Look at the titles of the readings and their brief descriptions to preview this unit's content. Before you begin each reading, answer the questions about it.

Reading 1

Vacationing in Space

Would you like to take a trip into space? This article makes some predictions about what it will be like.

1. How do you think traveling in space would be different from traveling on Earth?
2. When do you think it will be possible for ordinary people to travel in space?
3. If you could travel in space, what would you like to do there?

Reading 2

Ecotourism

Sometimes tourism harms the environment. However, *ecotourism* has a positive impact on the environment. This article describes three vacations for ecotourists that benefit local economies and environments.

1. If you could travel anywhere in the world, where would you like to go? Why?
2. What would you do on an ideal vacation?
3. In what ways can tourism harm the environment? In what ways can it benefit people?

Reading 3

Jet Lag

Jet lag often affects air travelers when they change time zones. This excerpt from a book looks at the problem.

1. Do you prefer to travel by car, plane, train, or ship? Why?
2. Have you ever traveled between time zones by plane? How did the trip affect you?
3. Do you think long-distance air travel affects everyone the same way? Explain your answer.

Vacationing in Space

Previewing Vocabulary

The words in the box are from the reading. Discuss the meanings of the words with a partner. Look up any new words in a dictionary. Then write each word in the correct column.

accommodations	cosmic	destination	forest fire	orbit
planets	spacecraft	universe	volcano	zero gravity

Words related to space	Words related to travel	Words related to Earth

Scanning

Scan the reading for the words in the box to check your answers. Then read the whole text.

1 Soon vacationers will have an exciting new possibility: space tourism. Today, it is possible for ordinary people to travel in space, but it certainly isn't common. However, some companies are planning ahead.

2 What accommodations will tourists need in space? Where will they eat and sleep after they have arrived at their destination? Tourists will stay in specially designed space hotels.

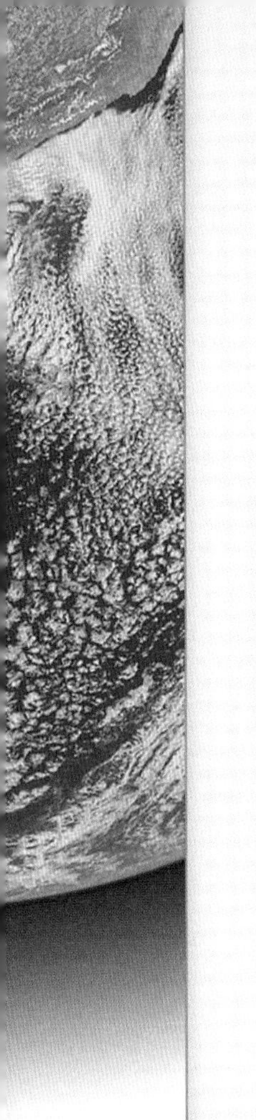

The first ones will probably be simple, individual modules that are linked together. As tourism increases, these structures will be developed into grand hotels.

What activities will space hotels offer? There are plans to build huge space stadiums 3
where people can enjoy water sports and various ball games. Imagine swimming or playing ball in zero gravity! As the number of space tourists grows, hotels will develop other kinds of entertainment as well.

Surveys show that the first thing most people want to do in space is look at Earth. 4
As you orbit Earth, the view is constantly changing. You see mountains, deserts, oceans, rivers, clouds, and even city lights at night. You might also see an active volcano or a forest fire. If the weather conditions are right, you could get a bird's eye view of the aurora borealis.[1]

Space vacations will cost money, of course, but you won't be able to bring the forms 5
of payment we use on Earth. You can't use cash because any coins with sharp edges could damage people or equipment. Credit and debit cards won't work because cosmic radiation[2] would destroy their magnetic strips.

The foreign exchange company Travelex believes it has the answer. They have 6
developed a form of money called the QUID – Quasi Universal Intergalactic Denomination. The QUID is made of a special kind of plastic and has no dangerous sharp edges. QUIDs look like elliptical candies, with different colors and sizes used for different values. Each one has the image of the eight planets in the universe.

Travelex has also developed a new kind of wallet to carry QUIDs and to prevent them 7
from floating around inside the gravity-free areas of a spacecraft. The QUIDs are stacked on top of each other in the wallet, which is fastened at the top with Velcro.

Do you like the idea of a space vacation? Start saving now. Soon you'll be able to 8
buy QUIDs online and at money exchanges and pay for them with any of the world's currencies. Then all you'll have to do is reach for your space wallet and go!

---

[1] ***aurora borealis:*** lights that sometimes appear in the night sky in the most northern parts of the world

[2] ***radiation:*** extremely strong energy from heat or light

A Comprehension Check

Every paragraph is about one topic. Write the number of the correct paragraph next to each topic.

_____ a. This paragraph describes why you can't use regular money in space.

_____ b. This paragraph describes how people will carry money in space.

_____ c. This paragraph describes the money people will use in space.

_____ d. This paragraph describes the kinds of things people will do.

_____ e. This paragraph invites the reader to consider a space vacation.

_____ f. This paragraph says that in the future more people are going to travel in space.

_____ g. This paragraph describes the parts of Earth you can see from space.

_____ h. This paragraph describes where people will stay.

B Vocabulary Study

Find the words in *italics* in the reading. Then match each sentence with the correct picture.

a. These have *sharp edges*.	d. These are *stacked* on top of each other.
b. These have *magnetic strips*.	e. These are *fastened* together.
c. These are *elliptical* in shape.	f. These are *currencies*.

____ 1. 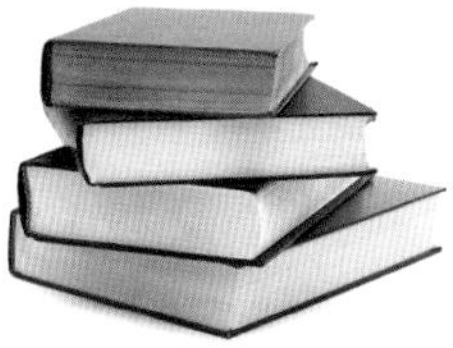

____ 3. 

____ 5. 

____ 2. 

____ 4. 

____ 6. 

C Understanding Pronoun Reference

Writers use different kinds of pronouns to refer to information that is stated earlier in a text. Some common pronouns are *it*, *one*, *they*, *them*, and *their*. Understanding pronoun reference is very important for reading comprehension.

What do these pronouns in *italics* refer to? Circle the letter of the correct answer.

1. *it* (par. 1, line 2)	a. travel in space	b. space
2. *they* (par. 2, line 1)	a. accommodations	b. tourists
3. *ones* (par. 2, line 3)	a. tourists	b. space hotels
4. *their* (par. 5, line 4)	a. sharp edges	b. credit or debit cards
5. *one* (par. 6, line 5)	a. QUID	b. candy
6. *them* (par. 8, line 2)	a. QUIDs	b. money exchanges

D Relating Reading to Personal Experience

Discuss these questions with your classmates.

1. Would you like to take a space vacation like the one described in the reading? Why or why not?
2. If you were going to take a trip in space, what would you take with you?
3. If you could design a space hotel, what would it look like?

Ecotourism

Thinking About the Topic

Check (✓) the things that you think ecotourists can do to help the local economy and not harm the environment. Compare your answers with a partner.

_____ 1. drive around the countryside

_____ 2. eat local food

_____ 3. help farmers work on their farm

_____ 4. hike in the jungle

_____ 5. stay in an air-conditioned luxury hotel

_____ 6. take a bicycle tour

_____ 7. visit archaeological sites

_____ 8. visit a wildlife reserve

Skimming

Skim the reading to check your answers. Then read the whole text.

Travel allows us to explore different places and learn about different cultures. But 1
today many tourists want to have a positive impact on the places they visit. They believe that it's important to respect the local people, help the local economy, and avoid harming the environment. These are the goals of the movement called "ecotourism." Interested tourists can find a variety of ecotourism destinations.

In Piedra Blanca, Ecuador, for example, you can experience life with a local family, 2
visit a village market, and help farmers pick crops, such as coffee, cacao (chocolate), sugar cane, and fruit. With a local guide, you can tour the rain forest, hike in the jungle, or ride a horse in the countryside. You can also visit archaeological sites. Much of the money that visitors spend on accommodations, food, and guides goes to a community fund, so the local people benefit.

3 Punta Laguna on Mexico's Yucatan peninsula is a village of Mayans[1] who participate in ecotourism. The men take turns guiding visitors through the large wildlife reserve that protects the local monkeys, birds, and other animals. They also take tourists on hikes in the jungle or on canoe trips. Similarly, the women take turns selling their crafts, including traditional clothing, wall hangings, and jewelry. In this way, everyone in the community shares in the profits from tourism.

4 In New Zealand, you can take a two-week bicycle tour that includes visiting glaciers and seeing ocean wildlife. Bicycling is an ideal way to tour without harming the environment. You can also tour a farm where you can watch sheep shearing and help with tasks such as milking cows. If you prefer, you can travel through the Marlborough Sounds with a Maori[2] family on their boat. You will learn about the sea animals and birds you see. You will sleep and eat on the boat and visit with other Maori along the way. You will experience a different culture and at the same time, contribute to the tourism that is so important for the Maori economy.

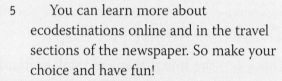

5 You can learn more about ecodestinations online and in the travel sections of the newspaper. So make your choice and have fun!

[1] ***Mayans:*** a native people of Mexico
[2] ***Maori:*** the native people of New Zealand

A Comprehension Check

Check (✓) the places where you can do the activities.

	Piedra Blanca	Punta Laguna	New Zealand
1. buy things at a local market			
2. go for a hike			
3. have a local guide show you the area			
4. help the local economy			
5. live on a boat			
6. ride a horse			
7. see wildlife			
8. spend time on a farm			
9. stay with a local family			

B Vocabulary Study

Find the words in the box in the reading. Then complete the sentences.

explore (par. 1)	avoid (par. 1)	participate (par. 3)
take turns (par. 3)	profits (par. 3)	contribute (par. 4)

1. If you want to ________________, please tell us now. We can't take everyone on the tour.
2. You need to ________________. Today you stay on the boat, and tomorrow your brother will stay on the boat.
3. What should we do with the ________________? How should we use the money we made?
4. If you want to ________________ to the local economy, you should buy things from the local people.
5. You don't learn much about a place if you don't ________________ it.
6. I don't want to harm the environment, so I ________________ doing anything that will be bad for it.

C Recognizing Point of View

Sometimes a writer expresses a point of view, or an opinion. It is important for readers to be able to recognize the presence of a point of view and to understand what that point of view is.

Check (✓) the statement that best expresses the writer's point of view. Discuss the reason for your answer with a partner.

____ 1. The writer thinks all kinds of travel, including ecotourism, are good.

____ 2. The writer doesn't think ecotourism is for everybody.

____ 3. The writer thinks ecotourism is a good thing.

____ 4. The writer thinks people should only travel to ecotourism destinations.

D Relating Reading to Personal Experience

Discuss these questions with your classmates.

1. Which of the trips mentioned in the reading would you like to take? Why?
2. Imagine that you want to take an ecotourism vacation. What do you need to think about when you're planning your trip? For example, what is the climate like? What do you need to bring with you?
3. If someone wanted to come to your country on an ecotourism vacation, what places would you suggest for them to visit?

Jet Lag

Predicting

Look at the subheadings in the reading. Then check (✓) what you think the main idea of the reading is. Compare your answers with a partner.

_____ 1. The reading is about how people feel when jet lag affects them.

_____ 2. The reading is about why people get jet lag.

_____ 3. The reading is about what people can do to avoid getting jet lag.

_____ 4. The reading is about why people should try not to get jet lag.

Skimming

Skim the reading to check your answer. Then read the whole text.

1 There is one thing that can ruin vacations, make business meetings less than successful, and cause more problems than anything else for air travelers. Jet lag! Jet lag affects nearly everyone who takes a long flight.

2 Jet lag results from traveling a long distance to a new time zone. The travel time is too fast for the human body to adjust easily. Long-distance air travel to a new time zone

disrupts three important senses: the sense of place, the sense of time, and, as a result of both, the sense of well-being.

Sense of place: To some extent, all locations are geographically and even chemically different from one another. Humans, like all living things, have a strong sense of place. This makes people homesick for familiar surroundings and wish for their own bed. 3

Sense of time: We all also have a natural sense of time that is linked to our sense of place. Our bodies function on a program that takes about a day to run, and they sense the different qualities of dawn, noon, and midnight. This is why travel to a distant time zone makes us miss the usual hometown patterns of something as simple as the times of sunrise and sunset. When familiar patterns such as these are interrupted, it affects the way we feel. 4

Sense of well-being: We have a sense of well-being when we are healthy and happy. This sense is strongly connected to our senses of place and time. That is why flying to a new environment and time zone often causes a disruption in our sense of well-being. 5

For thousands of years, people didn't experience disruption in their sense of time and place because there were no rapid means of transportation. They could only go as fast as their feet could take them, their animals could carry them, or their boats could transport them. It took weeks, months, years, or even generations to travel great distances. 6

The invention of the airplane changed all this. However, although we can travel by plane now, our bodies have not yet adapted to long-distance air travel. That is why we suffer the consequences – jet lag. 7

Adapted from *Overcoming Jet Lag*

A Comprehension Check

Look at the example. Then find and correct five more mistakes in the paragraphs.

People get jet lag when they travel ~~short~~ long distances by plane. Humans don't have a very strong sense of place. For this reason, sometimes we don't feel well when we travel to new places too slowly. We also get used to what the different times of day are like in the place where we live: the mornings, the afternoons, and the nights. Therefore, when we fly somewhere far away, our sense of place is also disrupted.

For thousands of years, people did not have jet lag because they didn't travel short distances quickly. The airplane changed that, but our minds haven't had time to adapt yet. So today our sense of well-being is often affected when we travel long distances by plane to different time zones.

B Vocabulary Study

Find the words in *italics* in the reading. Then match the words with their meanings.

____ 1. *ruin* (par. 1)	a. stops something from continuing as usual
____ 2. *adjust* (par. 2)	b. continue until the end
____ 3. *disrupts* (par. 2)	c. affect something so that it becomes bad
____ 4. *chemically* (par. 3)	d. change a little to make something work well
____ 5. *surroundings* (par. 3)	e. the place and conditions in which you live
____ 6. *run* (par. 4)	f. related to changes in the atoms or molecules of substances

C Recognizing Cause and Effect

When you read, it is important to recognize the reason why something happens (the cause). It is also important to recognize what happens as a result (the effect).

Use the information in the reading to decide whether each statement below is a cause of jet lag or an effect of jet lag. Write *C* (cause) or *E* (effect).

__C__ 1. The travel time is too fast for people to adjust easily.

____ 2. People's vacations are ruined.

____ 3. People wish for their own bed.

____ 4. People's sense of time is connected to their sense of place.

____ 5. A business meeting is not successful.

____ 6. People's bodies have not changed for thousands of years.

D Relating Reading to Personal Experience

Discuss these questions with your classmates.

1. Do you think jet lag is a serious problem? Why or why not?
2. Do you know any ways to avoid jet lag? Explain your answer.
3. What other things can ruin a plane trip besides jet lag?

Reread one of the unit readings and time yourself. Note your reading speed in the chart on page 124.

UNIT 7

The Internet

Look at the titles of the readings and their brief descriptions to preview this unit's content. Before you begin each reading, answer the questions about it.

Reading 1

Love on the Internet

Do you want to get married? Why not look online for Ms. or Mr. Right? In this article, find out how people use the Internet as a matchmaking service.

1. For a happy marriage, which should both spouses have: the same roots, the same lifestyle, the same background?
2. In your culture, what are the traditional ways of meeting someone if you want to get married?
3. Would you use the Internet to help you find a spouse? Why or why not?

Reading 2

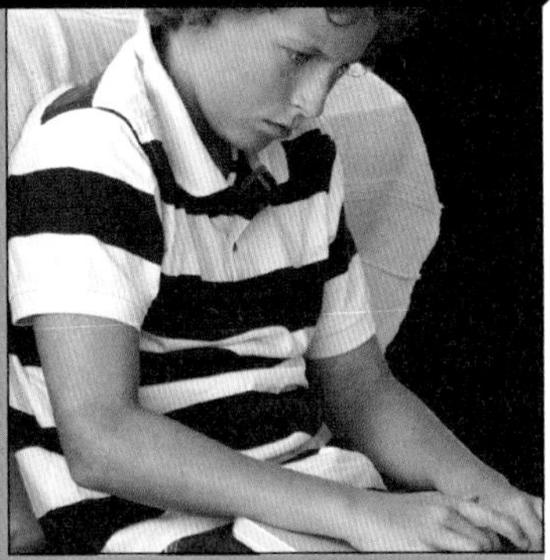

Help on the Internet

This magazine article tells the remarkable true story of how someone's life was saved with the help of the Internet.

1. Do you ever visit Internet chat rooms? If so, which ones?
2. Would you believe the stories of someone you met in an Internet chat room? Why or why not?
3. Imagine you are home alone and suddenly feel ill. How could the Internet help you?

Reading 3

How Wikis Work

Today more and more people are going online, and especially to wikis, for information. In this article, find out how wikis work.

1. Where do you look when you want information – for example, information about an event in history or an interesting quote for a project or report?
2. How often do you use wikis? If you use them often, which is your favorite one?
3. In what ways is information online better than information in printed books? In what ways is it worse?

Love on the Internet

Thinking About What You Know

Check (✓) the advantages of looking for a spouse on the Internet. Compare your answers with a partner.

_____ 1. You can get to know all about a person.

_____ 2. You can find out easily if you and the other person have chemistry.

_____ 3. You can get replies quickly.

_____ 4. You are in control.

_____ 5. You can select possible candidates from a large group of people.

_____ 6. If you wish, you can be anonymous so that no one knows who you are.

Skimming

Skim the reading to see if your answers match the advantages that the writer discusses. Then read the whole text.

1 Caught between his traditional Muslim roots and his Californian lifestyle, Tariq Ahmed found the perfect way to arrange his own marriage. He went online. Tariq, a Silicon Valley computer expert, was born in London to a Pakistani father and an Austrian mother. Along with thousands of other young people whose families come from Southern Asia, he looked at the growing number of Internet sites dedicated to finding a suitable husband or wife.

2 As a designer of web pages, Tariq had little difficulty producing his own site. He admits that, like many of his friends from traditional backgrounds, he had to do something about his love life. Tariq said that his dad was very conservative, and "he just wanted me to marry a Muslim girl."

She turned out to be Juliana Gidwani. She saw Tariq's advertisement on the Internet, and their relationship began. They eventually got married near her home in Singapore. The wedding pictures, of course, were immediately posted on the Web. 3

Tariq thinks "the Internet isn't ideal because you have to use e-mails, and when you are talking in text you are only getting a bit of information." He adds that e-mails can't show whether there is chemistry between two people. Luckily, after he and his bride spent time getting to know each other, they discovered that they did have chemistry. 4

Kumar Kakumanu, a New York-based Indian born in Hyderabad, has been in the United States for more than 10 years. Now he is looking for an Indian wife on the Web. He wants to find someone "with a cosmopolitan[1] outlook." Kumar thinks the Internet works well, even though you can't get all the information you need. He says, "With the Internet it is possible to specifically target or broaden your search criteria.[2] Traditional methods are just too slow." 5

Sara was born in India and is studying in the United States. She is another example of someone who thinks the Internet is a good way to find a spouse. After her parents' matchmaking attempts failed, she began her own search. She registered with an Indian agency on the Internet, and she had many replies. She quickly found a possible husband. "He's a doctor, a real golden boy with a flood of proposals from good families, which his parents have gone nuts trying to get him to accept." 6

Speed and control are what is important on the Internet. Web sites and e-mail allow people to choose the level of anonymity they wish to keep. In addition, on the Internet, people searching for spouses can do in days what once took months: exchange pictures, select the best candidates, and check each other's backgrounds. 7

---

[1] ***cosmopolitan:*** having experiences of different people and places

[2] ***search criteria:*** specific things that you are looking for

Adapted from *The Times*

A Comprehension Check

Fill in the missing information in the paragraphs.

Tariq Ahmed was born in ________________ (1). He was living in ________________ (2) when he decided to look for a wife on the Internet. His father wanted him to marry a ________________ (3) girl. Through the Internet, he met and married ________________ ________________ (4). She was living in ________________ (5) at the time.

Kumar Kakumanu is living in ________________ (6), but he is from ________________ (7). He is searching the Web for a wife from ________________ (8).

Sara was born in ________________ (9) and is living in the United States. Her ________________ (10) tried to find a spouse for her but didn't succeed. She registered with an Indian agency on the ________________ (11). She found one possible husband who is a ________________ (12).

B Vocabulary Study

Find the words and phrases in *italics* in the reading. Then circle the letters of the correct meanings.

1. *suitable* (par. 1)
   a. wrong for someone
   b. right for someone
2. *conservative* (par. 2)
   a. wanting things the same as before
   b. preferring new ways of doing things
3. *ideal* (par. 4)
   a. fast
   b. perfect
4. *outlook* (par. 5)
   a. a way of looking outside
   b. a way of thinking about something
5. *a flood of* (par. 6)
   a. many
   b. some
6. *have gone nuts* (par. 6)
   a. have eaten something
   b. have been excited about something

C Making Inferences

Sometimes the reader must infer, or figure out, what the writer did not explain or state directly in a text.

Check (✓) the statements that you can infer are true according to the reading.

_____ 1. Tariq and his wife are happily married.

_____ 2. Tariq's father was happy about Tariq's marriage.

_____ 3. Kumar's parents are helping him find a wife.

_____ 4. Kumar wants to marry someone who is familiar with different kinds of people.

_____ 5. Sara was unhappy because her parents tried to help her find a husband.

_____ 6. Sara has many attractive qualities.

D Relating Reading to Personal Experience

Discuss these questions with your classmates.

1. Would you marry someone that you met on the Internet without also having face-to-face meetings? Why or why not?
2. Imagine that you are looking for a spouse on the Internet. What search criteria would you use? What information would you give about yourself?
3. How long do you think people should know each other before they get married? Why?

Help on the Internet

Predicting

Look at the title, the picture, and the words and phrases in the box. What do you think happens in the story? Discuss your ideas with a partner.

chat room	Mom	Texas	international telephone operator
"What's wrong?"	college library	web name	emergency workers
paralyzed	Finland	local police	medical treatment

Skimming

Skim the reading to check your prediction. Then read the whole text.

One day, 12-year-old Sean Redden logged on to the Internet and went to a popular 1
chat room. Just as he was about to sign off and do something else, he saw the name of someone he'd never seen there before, Susan Hicks. Her brief message was "Would someone help me?"

Sean typed back, "What's wrong?" A moment later he received this message, "I can't 2
breathe. Help me! I can't feel my left side. I can't get out of my chair."

Oh, man, Sean thought. Pretending to be paralyzed was a bad joke. Then he wondered, 3
What if she really is sick? I've got to help. "Hey, Mom," he called. "There's a kid here who's sick or something."

Sharon Redden looked at the computer screen. "It's not just some game, is it?" 4
she asked.

The message was not a joke. "Susan Hicks" was actually 20-year-old Taija Laitinen, a 5
student working late at night at a college library near Helsinki, Finland – almost 7,000 miles away from Sean's home in Texas. While searching the Internet, she began to feel

terrible pain all through her body. What could she do? The library was silent and empty. The nearest phone was outside in the hallway. She couldn't move that far. Any movement caused the pain to get worse.

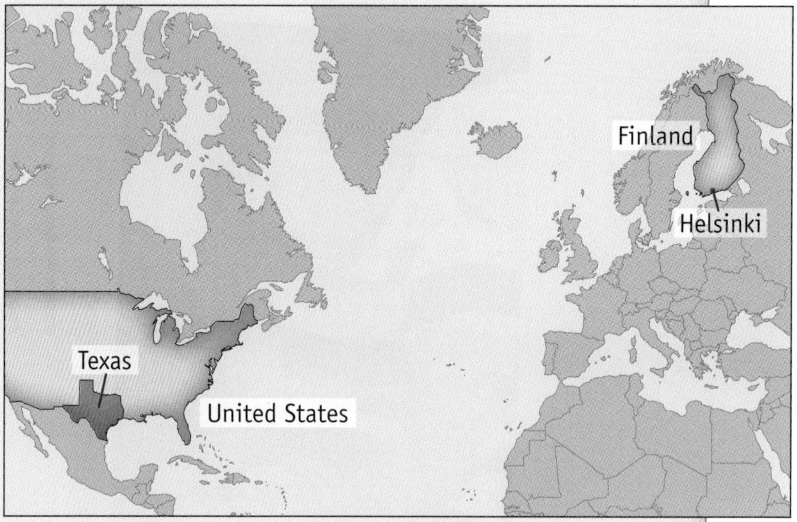

6 Then she realized that she might get help on the Internet. But how? Taija sometimes practiced her English in the chat room. As the pain got worse, she logged on using her web name and began typing her message for help.

7 "I don't think it's a joke, Mom," Sean said. He looked at Susan's last message, and he typed, "Where are you?" After a long pause, the letters appeared: "Finland." Sean and Sharon couldn't believe it. Not knowing what else to do, Sharon called the local police.

8 Sharon explained the situation to officer Amy Schmidt. Schmidt told Sharon to try to get the sick girl's phone number.

9 Sean asked several times for the girl's phone number and location. Finally, a message with her number and address came back. Texas police called the international telephone operator and asked to be connected to the proper agency in Finland. The call was transferred to a nearby rescue station. The Texas police explained the situation and gave Susan's address to the Finnish operator. When Sean heard that, he typed, "Help is on the way."

10 In a few minutes, Taija heard people running down the hallway outside the door. Suddenly, the door opened. Emergency workers and three policemen ran in. Taija turned once more to the computer, "They are here. Thanks. Bye-bye."

11 Four days later, the police in Texas received a message from officers in Finland: "Thanks to her Internet friend, Taija had received medical treatment she badly needed and is doing well."

Adapted from *Reader's Digest*

A Comprehension Check

Correct the mistake in each statement. The first one is marked for you.

1. At first, Sean ~~believed~~ didn't believe that the person sending the message for help was really sick.
2. Susan Hicks was a friend of Taija Laitinen.
3. Susan went on the Internet that day to practice her English.
4. Susan didn't phone for help because she didn't want to walk to the nearest phone.
5. Sean didn't know help was coming before Susan told him help had arrived.
6. Susan got medical treatment for an illness that was not serious.

B Vocabulary Study

Find the words and phrases in the box in the reading. Then complete the sentences.

logged on (par. 1)	sign off (par. 1)	realized (par. 6)
transferred (par. 9)	on the way (par. 9)	thanks to (par. 11)

1. ________________ you, I'm OK now. It was great of you to help me.
2. Two police officers are ________________. Just wait for them.
3. She went to the chat room and ________________, but she didn't see anything.
4. At first, he didn't know what to do, but then he ________________ that he could call the police.
5. I can't help you, but I ________________ your call to someone who can.
6. When you want to leave the chat room, don't forget to ________________.

C Understanding the Order of Events

Understanding the order of events in a text means that you know what happens first, second, third, and so on. This information helps you understand the ideas in the text.

Number the sentences from *1* (first event) to *10* (last event). The first one is marked for you.

____ a. The Texas police called the international operator.

____ b. Sean's mother called the police in Texas.

__1__ c. Sean logged on to the Internet.

____ d. Sean began receiving messages from someone named "Susan."

____ e. "Susan" heard footsteps outside her door.

____ f. Sean found out where "Susan" was.

____ g. The international operator connected the Texas police to the police in Finland.

____ h. Sean showed his mother that someone on the Internet was asking for help.

____ i. Sean entered a chat room.

____ j. Sean received a message that said that help had arrived.

D Relating Reading to Personal Experience

Discuss these questions with your classmates.

1. Imagine that Sean had called the Texas police instead of his mother. Do you think the police would have acted differently? Why or why not?
2. Do you think Sean and Taija still communicate with each other? Why or why not?
3. Do you use the Internet to practice English? If so, how? If not, would you like to?

How Wikis Work

Thinking About the Topic

How much do you know about wikis? Check (✓) the statements that you think are true. Then compare your answers with a partner.

_____ 1. Anyone can add or change information on a wiki.

_____ 2. It is easy to create a wiki.

_____ 3. Each wiki has one or two editors who review the articles and check them for errors.

_____ 4. All the information on wikis is reliable.

_____ 5. Different wikis have different kinds of content.

_____ 6. Information is updated on wikis all the time.

Skimming

Skim the reading to find which of the statements are true. Then read the whole text.

1 *Wiki* is the Hawaiian word for "quick." Today, this term is becoming a very familiar word among Internet users. What does it mean? A wiki is a Web site that people can add to and change quickly and easily. All you need is a computer, a web browser, and access to the Internet. The most famous wiki is Wikipedia, an online encyclopedia that contains more than a million articles. But there are lots of other wikis such as WikiHow, Wikinews, and Wiktionary. They all have one thing in common. They are created and managed by a wiki community.

2 A wiki community is made up of the millions of people who visit a wiki site. Many of the visitors are readers looking for information. Some visitors are also writers who create articles for the site. Other visitors also act as editors who review the articles and check them for errors. Wikis are simple to create and use, and they are becoming increasingly popular.

3 But is wiki information reliable? If anyone can add, delete, or change information, can the information be trusted? This depends on the wiki community. The community usually tries to make sure that the information on a topic is valid. If someone who is knowledgeable about a topic sees an entry with inaccurate information, that person can edit, or change, it.

4 Changes to wiki entries on a site can be accepted, revised, or rejected by the site's community. In that way, pages on wiki sites are expanding and changing all the time. In fact, on a big wiki like Wikipedia, thousands of pages change every day. At certain times of the day there can be 50 or more pages changing every minute! Sometimes the changes may be as simple as a corrected spelling or grammatical error. Other times they are changes or additions to the content.

5 A wiki is a collaborative project. It can be created for any topic that has an active community of people who are interested in it. Do you want to find an interesting quote to use in a writing project or report? Go to Wikiquotes. Do you want to learn the most recent information about a place you're planning to visit? Try Wikitravel. A wiki gives the community a way to gather information together and modify it as things change. Wikis are dramatically changing the way we get information. And unlike information in a printed book, the information is being updated all the time.

A Comprehension Check

Circle the letter of the statement that best expresses the main idea of each paragraph.

1. Paragraph 1
   a. Wikipedia is the most famous wiki.
   b. A wiki is a Web site that people can add to and change quickly.
   c. All wikis have a wiki community.

2. Paragraph 2
   a. A wiki community has millions of people.
   b. Wikis are becoming more and more popular.
   c. In a wiki community, people use the wiki to get or create information.

3. Paragraph 3
   a. People can change and add information when they want.
   b. There are possible problems with wikis.
   c. Wiki communities try to make sure that the information on their site is accurate.

4. Paragraph 4
   a. Sometimes grammar or spelling is corrected.
   b. The information in a wiki changes all the time.
   c. Sometimes more than 50 pages change in a minute.

5. Paragraph 5
   a. In a wiki community, people with similar interests work together.
   b. Wikitravel is a good wiki for information about a place you are going to visit.
   c. Wikis are very different from books.

B Vocabulary Study

Find the words in *italics* in the reading. Are the meanings of the words in each pair similar or different? Write *S* (similar) or *D* (different).

__S__ 1. *contains* (par. 1) / *is made up of* (par. 2)

____ 2. *becoming . . . familiar* (par. 1) / *expanding* (par. 4)

____ 3. *reliable* (par. 3) / *trusted* (par. 3)

____ 4. *valid* (par. 3) / *inaccurate* (par. 3)

____ 5. *revised* (par. 4) / *corrected* (par. 4)

____ 6. *collaborative* (par. 5) / *knowledgeable* (par. 3)

____ 7. *modify* (par. 5) / *change* (par. 5)

C Recognizing Point of View

Sometimes a writer expresses a point of view, or an opinion. It is important for readers to be able to recognize the presence of a point of view and to understand what that point of view is.

Check (✓) the statement that best expresses the writer's point of view. Discuss the reason for your answer with a partner.

____ 1. It is easier to change the information in wikis than in books, so in the future books will not be necessary.

____ 2. People shouldn't use wikis because the information is not always correct.

____ 3. Everyone should be part of a wiki community.

____ 4. Wikis are not perfect, but they can be an excellent source of information.

D Relating Reading to Personal Experience

Discuss these questions with your classmates.

1. Which of the wikis mentioned in the reading have you used? What kind of information do you use them for?
2. People can put anything that they want on the Internet. Is this a problem or is it a good thing? Explain your answer.
3. If you could create a wiki for something that you are really interested in, what kinds of information would be on the wiki?

Reread one of the unit readings and time yourself. Note your reading speed in the chart on page 124.

UNIT 8

Friends

Look at the titles of the readings and their brief descriptions to preview this unit's content. Before you begin each reading, answer the questions about it.

Reading 1

Ten Easy Ways to Make Friends

This magazine article offers some practical advice on how to make new friends.

1. Do you find it easy or difficult to make new friends? Explain your answer.
2. What qualities does a good friend have?
3. What do you and your friends have in common?

Reading 2

Best Friends

What does it mean to have a best friend? In this introduction to a book called *Best Friends*, the writer shares her ideas on this question.

1. How is a best friend different from all other friends?
2. Are friendships between males different from friendships between females? If so, how?
3. How are friendships different from family relationships?

Reading 3

Are Online Friends Real Friends?

The writer of this article discusses the advantages and disadvantages of having friends that you meet through the Internet.

1. How many online friends do you have? What do you chat about with them?
2. Do you think it's easier to make friends online or face-to-face? Explain your answer.
3. What are some social networking sites or chat rooms that you know about? Do you visit any of them? If so, which ones? If not, why not?

Ten Easy Ways to Make Friends

Previewing Vocabulary

The words in the box are from the reading. Discuss the meanings of these words with a partner. Look up any new words in a dictionary. Decide which words describe the qualities of a good friend.

caring	consistent	generous	popular
self-critical	shy	supportive	talkative

Scanning

Scan the reading to find the words in the box. Circle those qualities, which according to the writer are the qualities of a good friend. Then read the whole text.

1 It's hard to make friends if you stay home alone all the time. You need to get out of the house and do things that will help you meet other people. Join a club, play a sport, do volunteer work. You'll find that it's easier to make friends with people who have similar interests.

2 Learn from people at school or work who seem to make friends easily. Observe their behavior. How do they make other people feel comfortable? Notice what they say and

how they act. Don't copy everything they do, but try some of their techniques. It will help you develop your own social style.

Don't be afraid to show people what you're really good at. Talk about the things that 3
you like and do best. You might excel in sports, school, the arts, science, or some other area. People will want to learn about your interests and your strong points.

Think of some topics that would make good conversation. Find out the latest news, 4
listen to the most popular types of music, or watch an interesting movie or TV show. The more you have to say, the more people will want to talk with you.

Be a good listener, and let people talk about themselves. Don't try to dominate the 5
conversation with "me, me, me." Ask lots of questions. Show an interest in the answers. This will make people feel special, and they will want to be your friend.

Look people in the eye when you talk to them. It's hard to have a conversation when 6
your eyes are looking everywhere except at the other person's face. If you don't make eye contact, people may think you're not interested in them. As a result, they may stop being interested in you.

When you start to get to know someone, don't be friendly and talkative one day and 7
too shy to have a conversation the next day. Be consistent. Consistency is a quality that people look for in friends.

Have confidence in yourself. Don't be self-critical all the time. It's hard to get other 8
people to like you if you don't like yourself! Think of your good qualities and all the reasons people would want your friendship.

Pursue the friendships you really want, with people that you like, respect, and admire. 9
Try to meet a lot of people, too. That way, you'll have a bigger group to choose from and a better chance to make friends.

After you make new friends, keep them by being a good friend. Be loyal, caring, 10
supportive, and generous. It's likely that your friends will treat you in the same way.

Adapted from *Teen*

A Comprehension Check

Complete the chart with sentences from the box. Write the letters in the correct columns according to information in the reading.

a. ~~Look people in the eye.~~
b. Be loyal, caring, and supportive.
c. Be consistent.
d. Be a good listener.
e. Treat people the way you want to be treated.
f. Find out the latest news.
g. Join a club or play a sport.
h. Ask lots of questions.
i. Watch how other people make friends.

Before meeting new friends	When you're with new friends	After making new friends
	a	

B Vocabulary Study

Find the words and phrases in *italics* in the reading. Then circle the correct meanings.

1. When you *observe* something, you **write it down** / **watch it**. (par. 2)
2. Your *strong points* are your **good features** / **bad features**. (par. 3)
3. When you *dominate* a conversation, you want to **control** / **end** it. (par. 5)
4. When you *pursue* something, you **like** / **look for** it. (par. 9)
5. When you *admire* someone, you **have a good opinion of** / **love** the person. (par. 9)
6. When you are *loyal*, you **support** / **talk to** your friends all the time. (par. 10)

C Applying Information from the Text

When you read, you often learn new information. Applying information from a text to new situations shows that you understand the information well.

Read the statements about the people. What advice in the reading does each person need to follow? Write the correct paragraph number.

__4__ a. Tony is never sure what to talk about when he meets people.

_____ b. Rosa wants to know why her classmate, Susana, is so good at making friends.

_____ c. When Pedro feels uncomfortable talking to someone, he starts to look away.

_____ d. Yurika doesn't always say nice things about her new friend, Ivan.

_____ e. Hassan wants to be friends with Elena because she's popular.

_____ f. Adam stays home every Saturday night and watches TV.

_____ g. Ruby often asks herself, "Why would anyone want to be my friend?"

_____ h. Benson is a terrific dancer, but he never tells anyone about it.

_____ i. Marta always talks about herself.

_____ j. Ali talked to Kim on Monday, but on Tuesday he was afraid to say "Hi."

D Relating Reading to Personal Experience

Discuss these questions with your classmates.

1. What do you think is the most helpful advice in the reading?
2. Do you disagree with any of the advice? If so, why do you disagree?
3. Have you ever tried to follow one of the writer's suggestions? If so, did it work?

Best Friends

Predicting

Look at the title, the picture, and the phrases from the reading in the box. What do you think the writer's main focus is? Check (✓) the appropriate statement. Discuss your answer with a partner.

the family that we choose	never have to explain yourself
always there when you need them	will not judge you
lessens your sorrow	unconditional love

_____ 1. The writer talks about how she met her best friend.

_____ 2. The writer talks about the difference between a friend and a best friend.

_____ 3. The writer talks about the qualities of a best friend.

Skimming

Skim the reading to check your prediction. Then read the whole text.

In this introduction to her book, the writer explores why best friends are "the family that we choose."

Men and women define "best friend" in the same way – a person who is always there when you need them. Your best friend is someone who shares your happiness, suffers through your worries, and lessens your sorrow. As one man said, "A best friend is somebody that you call if you get a flat tire on the expressway at 3:00 a.m., and you have to wait hours for a tow truck. Your friend says, 'Tell me exactly where you are, and I'll come and get you.'" 1

2 A variety of factors can help establish a best friendship, including the age of the people, the situation in which they meet, and how they satisfy each other's needs. But in my study, I found the main themes that define a best friend were remarkably similar for many people.

3 "Safety" was a word I heard over and over. A best friend makes you feel safe and provides a comfort zone.[1] You never have to explain yourself to best friends because they understand you so well. You can be exactly who you are. You can cry too hard or laugh too loud and never worry about what they'll think. Best friends will give you advice if you want it and encouragement if you need it, but they will not judge you or make you ashamed of your behavior. A best friend gives you unconditional love. That means complete love, without any limits.

4 Best friends are loyal and trustworthy. A best friend is a person who you can tell your most embarrassing personal secrets to. You can be sure that your best friend won't repeat your secrets to anyone else. Best friends can also be completely honest with you, but in the most gentle way.

5 Finally, best friends are the family you choose. They love you because they want to, not because they have to. For many people, a best friend becomes the brother or sister they'd always wanted but never had.

6 A man I knew asked his dying mother, "What has been the most important thing in your life?" He fully expected her to say her husband, her children, or her family. Instead, without a moment's hesitation, she replied sweetly, "My friends."

---

[1] ***comfort zone:*** a situation in which you feel relaxed

Adapted from *Best Friends*

A Comprehension Check

Check (✓) the statements that are true according to the reading.

_____ 1. Best friends always help when there is a problem.

_____ 2. Best friends have similar interests.

_____ 3. Best friends really know each other.

_____ 4. People know their best friend will not tell anybody their secrets.

_____ 5. Best friends don't have arguments.

_____ 6. Best friends are like family.

B Vocabulary Study

Find the noun forms of the words in column A in the reading. Write the nouns in column B. Then match the nouns in column B with their meanings in column C.

A	B		C
1. *happy* **adj.**	happiness	(par. 1)	a. protection from bad things
2. *various* **adj.**	________	(par. 2)	b. the way people act
3. *safe* **adj.**	________	(par. 3)	c. pleasure
4. *encourage* **v.**	________	(par. 3)	d. different types of one thing
5. *behave* **v.**	________	(par. 3)	e. a pause before speaking
6. *hesitate* **v.**	________	(par. 6)	f. helping someone have confidence or hope

C Identifying Main Ideas and Supporting Details

Identifying the main ideas and supporting details in a text is an important strategy that will help your reading comprehension. It's a good idea to find the main ideas first. Then look for the supporting details that explain the main ideas more fully.

In the following list, find two main ideas from the reading and mark them *MI*. Find the details that support these main ideas and mark them *SD*. Then complete the sentences below by matching each *MI* with its two *SD*s.

MI 1. Men and women define "best friend" in the same way – a person who is always there when you need them.

____ 2. You can be exactly who you are.

____ 3. Your best friend is someone who shares your happiness, suffers through your worries, and lessens your sorrow.

____ 4. You never have to explain yourself to best friends because they understand you so well.

____ 5. A best friend will not judge you.

____ 6. Your friend says, "Tell me where exactly you are, and I'll come and get you."

Sentence ____ is a main idea. It is supported by details ____ and ____.

Sentence ____ is a main idea. It is supported by details ____ and ____.

D Relating Reading to Personal Experience

Discuss these questions with your classmates.

1. How long have you known your best friend (or a good friend)?
2. How did you meet this friend? Why do you think you are so close?
3. Which of the qualities in the reading are true for your relationship with your best friend?

Are Online Friends Real Friends?

Thinking About the Topic

Check (✓) the statements that you think are true. Compare your answers with a partner.

_____ 1. Making new friends through the Internet is convenient and fast.

_____ 2. Online friends can offer emotional support.

_____ 3. It's easier to deceive people online.

_____ 4. People sometimes exaggerate their good qualities to make you think that they're better than they really are.

_____ 5. Online friends often become face-to-face friends.

_____ 6. In the future, people will have more online friends than face-to-face friends.

Skimming

Skim the reading to find which statements the writer thinks are true. Then read the whole text.

1 Modern computer technology has made a new kind of human relationship possible: online friendship. Online friends, or virtual friends, are people who have become acquainted with each other through the Internet. Are online friendships as beneficial as face-to-face friendships? What are the advantages and disadvantages of having virtual friends? Can people form strong bonds online? Today these questions are the subject of lively debate.

Some people believe that the Internet is the best way to make new friends. It's convenient, it's fast, and it allows you to make contact with different kinds of people from all over the world. When you use social networking Web sites and chat rooms, you can easily find people with interests and hobbies similar to yours. Information updates and photos add to the experience. Making friends on the Internet is especially good for shy people who feel uncomfortable in social situations. It's often easier to share thoughts and feelings online. In addition, virtual friends can offer emotional support. They can make people feel less lonely and help them solve problems. 2

Although the Internet can encourage friendship, it has a major disadvantage. When you're not face-to face, it's much easier to deceive people. Online friends only tell you what they want you to know. They sometimes exaggerate their good qualities and hide the less positive ones, so you can't be sure of what they are really like. That is why you should not give personal information to anyone online unless you're totally sure of who that person is. 3

Can online friendships be as meaningful as face-to-face ones? There are different points of view. Researchers at the University of Southern California surveyed 2,000 households in the United States. The results showed that more than 40 percent of participants feel "as strongly about their online buddies" as they do about their "offline" friends. Researchers also found that it's not unusual for online friends to become face-to-face friends. In contrast, there are many people who believe that it's not possible to have deep relationships with online friends. A young Indian software engineer, Lalitha Lakshmipathy, says, "It's good to feel connected with many people, but all my e-buddies are not necessarily my close friends." Many people would agree. They say that it's hard to develop feelings of trust and connection when you don't share experiences in person. 4

People continue to express different opinions about online friendship. However, most of them would agree that virtual friendships must not replace face-to-face friendships. As one life coach[1] says, "a social networking site should only be the 'add on' in any relationship." 5

---

[1] ***life coach:*** someone who you pay to give you advice about how to improve your life

A Comprehension Check

Every paragraph is about one topic. Write the number of the correct paragraph next to each topic.

_____ a. This paragraph describes a problem with online friendships.

_____ b. This paragraph explains that face-to-face friendships will always be more important than online friendships.

_____ c. This paragraph discusses the advantages of online friendships.

_____ d. This paragraph lists questions that people have about online friendships.

_____ e. This paragraph discusses differences in how people feel about their online and face-to-face friends.

B Vocabulary Study

Match the words and phrases from the reading that are similar in meaning.

____ 1. *virtual friends* (par. 1)
____ 2. *beneficial* (par. 1)
____ 3. *face-to-face* (par. 1, 3–5)
____ 4. *deep relationships* (par. 4)
____ 5. *express* (par. 5)
____ 6. *opinions* (par. 5)

a. *strong bonds* (par. 1)
b. *good* (par. 2)
c. *points of view* (par. 4)
d. *e-buddies* (par. 4)
e. *say* (par. 4)
f. *in person* (par. 4)

C Paraphrasing

Paraphrasing a text means using your own words to say what you have read. This is one strategy that you can use to improve your understanding of a text.

Circle the letter of the best paraphrase for each statement from the reading.

1. *Information updates and photos add to the experience.* (par. 2)
   a. It's good that people can always put their most recent news and photos online.
   b. The most recent news and photos make social networking more interesting.
2. *Although the Internet can encourage friendship, it has a major disadvantage.* (par. 3)
   a. The Internet can help people make friends, but there is a big problem with it.
   b. You can make friends on the Internet even though it's not a good idea.
3. *Online friends only tell you what they want you to know.* (par. 3)
   a. Virtual friends do not tell you everything.
   b. Virtual friends tell you what you ask them.
4. *A social networking site should only be the "add on" in any relationship.* (par. 5)
   a. People should include social networking in all of their relationships.
   b. Social networking shouldn't be the only way you connect with a friend.

D Relating Reading to Personal Experience

Discuss these questions with your classmates.

1. Do you think the Internet is the best way to make new friends? Explain your answer.
2. Do you think that online friendships can be as meaningful as face-to-face ones? Why or why not?
3. What will happen if virtual friendships replace face-to-face friendships in the future?

Reread one of the unit readings and time yourself. Note your reading speed in the chart on page 124.

UNIT 9 Gifts

Look at the titles of the readings and their brief descriptions to preview this unit's content. Before you begin each reading, answer the questions about it.

Reading 1

Gift Giving

When do people usually give gifts? What are some gift-giving traditions? You can find out the answers to these and other questions in this excerpt from a book.

1. On what occasions do people in your culture give gifts: birthdays? weddings? anniversaries? religious ceremonies? holidays?
2. Who do you give gifts to most often? Who most often gives you gifts?
3. What was the last gift you received? Who was it from?

Reading 2

Modern Day Self-Sacrifice

When people give gifts, they sometimes have to make a sacrifice. The writer gives a good example in this letter to a radio program host.

1. Unselfish people think about others, not only about themselves. Who is the most unselfish person you know? Give an example of that person's unselfish behavior.
2. Has anyone ever made a sacrifice for you? If so, what was the sacrifice?
3. What are some things that usually make parents proud of their children?

Reading 3

Gift Cards

When it's difficult to choose a gift for someone, a gift card may be a good idea. This article discusses the advantages and disadvantages of gift cards.

1. What do you think about when you choose a gift for someone? For example, think of the last gift you gave someone. Why did you choose that gift?
2. Who do you know who is hard to please with a gift?
3. Have you ever given anyone a gift card instead of a regular gift? If so, why did you do that?

Gift Giving

Thinking About the Topic

Check (✓) the statements that you think are true. Compare your answers with a partner.

_____ 1. People give gifts in almost all societies.

_____ 2. If you receive a birthday gift from someone, that person usually expects a birthday gift from you.

_____ 3. Important people, such as presidents and prime ministers, usually bring gifts when they visit a foreign leader.

_____ 4. Modern gift giving is wasteful.

_____ 5. There is an emotional benefit for people who give gifts to each other.

Skimming

Skim the reading to find which statements the writer thinks are true. Then read the whole text.

1 People give gifts in almost all societies. Gifts mark anniversaries, religious festivals, rites of passage,[1] and other important occasions. Sometimes there are even special ceremonies for gift giving. Some gifts are expensive, or they may take months to create. Others are of less value, such as birthday cards. What do these different kinds of gifts and gift-giving occasions have in common?

[1] ***rite of passage:*** a ceremony or event that marks an important stage in someone's life

Gift giving is often a process of exchange. If you receive a birthday gift from someone, that person usually expects a birthday gift from you in return. A gift establishes or confirms a social obligation. In some cultures, there are complex rules about gift exchange. In Pakistan, for example, there is a rule for giving gifts on special occasions, such as a wedding. This tradition is called "taking giving." It works this way: You give the wedding couple a gift, and they "repay" you with a gift of slightly higher value. Then you give the couple another gift. This one should be worth the difference between the first two gifts, plus a little more. The gift exchange continues, following the same pattern. 2

Sometimes gift giving is a form of tribute. A tribute is a gift to a powerful leader or country from a less powerful one. In many ancient cultures, people made offerings to their leaders to show their loyalty. The Nubians in ancient Egypt are a good example. They brought gold to the Egyptian pharaohs, or kings. Traditions like these continue today in some parts of the word. In parts of Africa, for example, farmers may give gifts to the local chiefs to thank them for hospitality or protection. 3

Today ambassadors, presidents, and prime ministers usually bring gifts when they visit a foreign leader. This tradition is different from the tribute system. Leaders bring gifts to strengthen relationships between countries, not to emphasize the power of the gift receiver. 4

Gifts can also send special messages. For example, gifts can tell people that we are thinking of them and that we want them to feel special. Sometimes a gift reminds us of the giver. The gift keeps the memory of a special person and a special relationship alive. 5

There is no doubt about the positive side of gift giving. That is why some people don't agree with anthropologist Claude Lévi-Strauss. He believed that modern gift giving is very wasteful; however, studies have shown that this is not true. It is clear that there is an emotional benefit for people who exchange gifts. That is surely enough of a reason for the tradition to continue. 6

Adapted from *A Celebration of Customs and Rituals*

A Comprehension Check

Every paragraph is about one topic. Write the number of the correct paragraph next to each topic.

_____ a. This paragraph describes how gifts can improve relationships between countries.

_____ b. This paragraph suggests that people with negative opinions about gift giving are wrong.

_____ c. This paragraph names occasions when people give gifts around the world.

_____ d. This paragraph describes why people sometimes give gifts to more powerful people.

_____ e. This paragraph explains how gifts can be a form of communication.

_____ f. This paragraph explains the process of giving a gift and getting one back.

B Vocabulary Study

Find the words and phrases in *italics* in the reading. Are the meanings of the words and phrases in each pair similar or different? Write *S* (similar) or *D* (different).

_____	1. a. *gifts* (par. 1)	b. *offerings* (par. 3)
_____	2. a. *exchange* (par. 2)	b. *in return* (par. 2)
_____	3. a. *ancient* (par. 3)	b. *modern* (par. 6)
_____	4. a. *chiefs* (par. 3)	b. *leaders* (par. 4)
_____	5. a. *receiver* (par. 4)	b. *giver* (par. 5)
_____	6. a. *reminds* (par. 5)	b. *keeps the memory alive* (par. 5)

C Identifying Supporting Details

Sometimes writers use examples as supporting details. Some common signals of examples are *for example* and *such as*. If you can identify examples in a text, you will have a clearer understanding of the writer's main ideas.

Look back at the reading and find examples of the following.

1. a gift of less value: ______________________________ (par. 1)
2. a country with rules for gift-giving: ______________________________ (par. 2)
3. a special occasion: ______________________________ (par. 2)
4. ancient leaders who received tribute: ______________________________ (par. 3)
5. a part of the world where tribute is common today: ______________________________ (par. 3)
6. a special message that a gift can send: ______________________________ (par. 5)

D Relating Reading to Personal Experience

Discuss these questions with your classmates.

1. Are there any rules or special traditions for gift giving in your culture?
2. Do you prefer to receive gifts or to give them? Explain your answer.
3. Are there are any negative aspects of gift giving? For example, do you think it is wasteful?

Modern Day Self-Sacrifice

Predicting

Look at the title, the picture, and the words and phrases from the reading in the box. What do you think happens in the story? Discuss your ideas with a partner.

son	"To my wonderful mother"
dirt motorcycle	wanted a piano
the shiniest helmet	many hugs and kisses
a beautiful keyboard	the proudest mother

Skimming

Skim the reading to check your prediction. Then read the whole text.

Dear Dr. Laura,

I always enjoy listening to your radio program. I enjoyed your story about gift giving 1
and unselfish love. You doubted that such unselfish love exists in today's world. Well, I'm
here to give you hope.

I wanted to do something very special for my fifteen-year-old son, who has always 2
been the perfect child. He worked all summer to earn enough money to buy a used dirt
motorcycle. Then he spent hours and hours restoring it until it looked almost new.

I was so proud of him that I bought him the shiniest helmet and a riding outfit 3
to wear.

4 I could hardly wait for him to open up his gift. In fact, I barely slept the night before.

5 Upon waking, I went into the kitchen to start making the coffee and tea. When I looked into the living room, I saw a beautiful keyboard with a big red bow and a note: "To my wonderful mother, all my love, your son."

6 I was so astonished. It had been a long-standing joke in our household that I wanted a piano so that I could take lessons. My husband's response was "learn to play the piano, and I'll get you one."

7 I stood there shocked, crying a river, asking myself how my son could afford this extravagant gift.

8 Of course, everyone woke up, and my son was thrilled with my reaction. We kissed and hugged, and I immediately wanted him to open my special gift.

9 When he saw the helmet and outfit, he had a strange look on his face. Then I realized what had happened. He had sold the motorcycle to get me the keyboard.

10 Of course I was the proudest mother ever on that day, and my feet never hit the ground for a month.

11 So I wanted you to know, that kind of love still exists and lives even in the ever-changing world of me, me, me!

12 I thought you'd love to share this story with your listeners.

A very proud parent

13 P.S. The next day, my husband and I bought our son a new "used" shiny motorcycle.

Adapted from www.drlaura.com/letters

A Comprehension Check

Look at the example. Then find and correct six more mistakes in this paragraph.

The writer's ~~husband~~ son worked all summer to buy a used keyboard. He was a very good son, so the writer wanted to do something nice for him. She bought him a book and riding clothes. But before she gave him the gift, she saw his gift for her in the kitchen. It was a motorcycle. She was very happy. Then she asked her son to open his gift. When he saw it, he had a happy look on his face. That's when she realized that he didn't have the motorcycle any more. He had sold it to buy the gift for her. That made her very proud of the boy. The next day the son bought another motorcycle.

B Vocabulary Study

Find the words in *italics* in the reading. Then circle the correct meaning of each word.

1. *Restoring* something means you **take it to the store** / **fix it**. (par. 2)
2. An *outfit* is **clothing** / **special equipment**. (par. 3)
3. When you are *astonished*, you are **bored** / **surprised**. (par. 6)
4. A *long-standing* joke is **very old** / **hard to understand**. (par. 6)
5. An *extravagant* gift is **unusual** / **expensive**. (par. 7)
6. If you are *thrilled*, you feel very **sad** / **happy**. (par. 8)

C Paraphrasing

> **Paraphrasing means using your own words to say what you have read. This is one strategy that you can use to improve your understanding of a text.**

Circle the letter of the best paraphrase for each statement or phrase from the reading.

1. *I stood there shocked, crying a river.* (par. 7)
   a. I was so surprised that I sat down near a river and cried.
   b. I was so surprised that I cried a lot.
2. . . . *my feet never hit the ground for a month.* (par. 10)
   a. I ran a lot for a month.
   b. I was very, very happy.
3. . . . *that kind of love still exists and lives even in the ever-changing world* . . . (par. 11)
   a. The world changes, but unselfish love still exists, as it did before.
   b. We live and love in a world that never changes.
4. . . . *world of me, me, me!* (par. 11)
   a. a world where people think of themselves first
   b. a world where people think of others before they think of themselves

D Relating Reading to Personal Experience

Discuss these questions with your classmates.

1. What is the most special gift that you ever gave to someone? Why was it so special?
2. Which of your possessions would be hardest to give up for someone that you loved?
3. What are some examples of unselfish love in the world today?

Gift Cards

Predicting

Look at the pictures and the title of the reading. Then check (✓) the topics that you think you will read about. Compare your answers with a partner.

_____ 1. why people give gift cards

_____ 2. how gift cards work

_____ 3. why gift cards are good for stores

_____ 4. the use of gift cards by teenagers

_____ 5. where gift cards are popular

_____ 6. laws about gift cards

Skimming

Skim the reading to find which topics are and are not in the reading. Then read the whole text.

1 Have you ever had trouble trying to choose a gift? Perhaps you need a birthday present for a friend who is hard to please. Maybe you want to find a gift for a neighbor who you don't know very well. How about clothing? You might be worried about choosing the wrong size, color, or style for a niece or a nephew. Books or DVDs? You may not know enough about the person's likes, dislikes, and interests. And giving money may not seem right. Well, how about a gift card?

2 A gift card is a card that is issued by a particular store. It's worth a certain amount of money. It looks like a credit card, but it actually works like cash. A gift-card holder can spend the amount of money noted on the card in the store that issued it. These cards are big money makers for retail companies. One reason is that when gift-card holders go to the store, they often see other things to buy, and they end up spending more money than the gift card is worth. Unused cards are another big source of revenue. Companies make millions of dollars because large numbers of people never use their cards. They either lose them, forget about them, or decide that it's not worth the effort.

3 Gift cards are becoming extremely popular in many countries around the world. In the United States, they are one of the most popular types of gifts. Why? People love the convenience – cards are easy to buy and easy to use, either in the store or online. The recipient can select his or her own gift, and the giver does not have to worry about finding just the right thing.

4 Receiving a gift card, however, is not the same as receiving a gift. An actual gift is a better reminder of the person who gave it. It helps us appreciate the thought and effort that went into the choice. The message of a real gift is more likely to be, "I spent some time trying to find the right gift for you because I care about you."

5 Often a gift card does not convey the same message as an actual gift. It may seem to say, "I was in a hurry. I didn't have time to think about what you would really like." Some people think that it takes the thought out of giving. In today's busy world, gift cards are certainly convenient. However, they can make us forget the real purpose of giving gifts, which is to build a closer bond between the gift-giver and the gift-recipient.

A Comprehension Check

For each question, two of the answers are correct. Cross out the answer that is *not* correct.

1. Why is it sometimes a good idea to give someone a gift card?
   a. You don't have enough money for a gift.
   b. You don't know the person very well.
   c. It's not right to give the person money.
2. Why do stores like gift cards?
   a. People who get the gift cards often buy more things.
   b. People often never use their cards.
   c. People use money to buy the gift cards.
3. Why are gift cards becoming so popular?
   a. They are convenient.
   b. They mean the same thing to the recipient as a gift.
   c. The recipient can choose something that he or she wants.
4. Why is it often better to give an actual gift than a gift card?
   a. An actual gift shows more thought and effort.
   b. An actual gift reminds you of the person who gave it to you.
   c. People spend more money on an actual gift than a gift card.

B Vocabulary Study

Find the words and phrases in *italics* in the reading. Then match the words and phrases with their meanings.

____ 1. *issued* (par. 2)	a. real
____ 2. *source of revenue* (par. 2)	b. communicate
____ 3. *worth the effort* (par. 2)	c. given or produced
____ 4. *actual* (par. 4)	d. useful to try doing something
____ 5. *appreciate* (par. 4)	e. way of earning money
____ 6. *convey* (par. 5)	f. be thankful for

C Recognizing Cause and Effect

When you read, it is important to recognize the reason why something happens (the cause). It is also important to recognize what happens as a result (the effect).

Use the information in the reading to decide whether each statement is a cause of giving gift cards or an effect of giving gift cards. Write *C* (cause) or *E* (effect).

__C__ 1. Someone is hard to please.

____ 2. You don't know the person's size or the style of clothing they like.

____ 3. Companies make a lot of money on gift cards.

____ 4. Gift cards are easy to buy and use.

____ 5. You don't have time to think about what the person would really like.

____ 6. Sometimes we forget the purpose of giving gifts.

D Relating Reading to Personal Experience

Discuss these questions with your classmates.

1. Would you like to receive a gift card? Why or why not?
2. Who would you *not* want to give a gift card to? Why?
3. When do you think a gift of cash is appropriate? When is it inappropriate?

Reread one of the unit readings and time yourself. Note your reading speed in the chart on page 124.

UNIT 10 Emotions

Look at the titles of the readings and their brief descriptions to preview this unit's content. Before you begin each reading, answer the questions about it.

Reading 1

Do You Have a Sense of Humor?

What does it mean when we say someone has a sense of humor? This article from the Internet explains what a sense of humor is and why laughter is so important.

1. What makes you laugh?
2. How do you feel when you laugh?
3. Why do you think some people are better than others at telling jokes?

Reading 2

Envy: Is It Hurting or Helping You?

Envy can be a difficult emotion to deal with. Read this article to find out why.

1. What are some things that people typically envy?
2. Do you think that men and women are envious of different things? Explain your answer.
3. What do you think causes envy?

Reading 3

The Value of Tears

Some people cry easily. Other people try not to cry. This magazine article explains why we cry and why crying is not something to be ashamed of.

1. Do you cry easily? What causes you to cry? How do you feel after you cry?
2. Do you feel embarrassed when you cry in public? Why or why not?
3. How do you deal with stress? Does crying ever help?

Reading 1

Do You Have a Sense of Humor?

Thinking About the Topic

Circle the letter of the information that you agree with. Compare your answers with a partner.

1. Laughter is ____.
   a. good for your health
   b. bad for your health
2. A sense of humor is ____.
   a. something that we are born with
   b. something that we develop
3. The ability to tell jokes is ____.
   a. the most important part of a sense of humor
   b. only a small part of a sense of humor
4. A sense of humor requires ____.
   a. the ability to make people laugh
   b. the ability to see the funny side of life

Skimming

Skim the reading to find out which statements the writer agrees with. Then read the whole text.

1 Humor and laughter are good for us. There is increasing evidence that they can heal us physically, mentally, emotionally, and spiritually. In fact, every system of the body responds to laughter in some positive, healing way. So how can we get more laughter into our lives? Is it possible to develop a sense of humor? Psychologist and author, Steve Wilson, has some answers.

Many people believe that we are born with a sense of humor. They think, "either you've got it, or you don't." Dr. Wilson points out that this is false. What is true, however, is that we are born with the capacity to laugh and smile. 2

The parts of the brain and central nervous system that control laughing and smiling are mature at birth. However, that does not mean that infants have a sense of humor. (After all, when a baby laughs, we don't rush over and say, "That kid has a great sense of humor!") A sense of humor is something that you can develop over a lifetime. 3

Sometimes people think that they don't have a good sense of humor because they are not good joke tellers. Dr. Wilson reminds us that telling jokes is only one of many ways to express humor. He advises us to lose our inhibitions and try to laugh at ourselves. Then we will make others laugh, too. 4

A person who has a true sense of humor is willing and able to see the funny side of everyday life. One of the best definitions of a sense of humor is "the ability to see the nonserious element in a situation." Consider this sign from a store window: "Any faulty merchandise[1] will be cheerfully replaced with merchandise of equal quality." The store manager probably placed the sign in the window to impress customers with the store's excellent service. He had a serious purpose, but if you have a sense of humor, you will probably find the sign funny! As Dr. Wilson says, "a good sense of humor means that you don't have to be funny; you just have to see what's funny." 5

[1] ***faulty merchandise:*** something you buy that does not work

Adapted from www.LaughterClubs.com

A Comprehension Check

Mark each statement *T* (true) or *F* (false). Then correct the false statements. The first one is marked for you.

F 1. We ~~are not~~ are born with the ability to laugh and smile.

____ 2. Every system of our body responds to laughter.

____ 3. Humor can help us emotionally and spiritually.

____ 4. The brain and central nervous system control having a sense of humor.

____ 5. It is good for people to be able to laugh at themselves.

____ 6. A person with a sense of humor has to be funny.

B Vocabulary Study

Find the words in *italics* in the reading. Then circle the letters of the correct meanings.

1. *heal* (par. 1)
   a. make sick
   b. make well
2. *responds* (par. 1)
   a. answers
   b. reacts
3. *mature* (par. 3)
   a. not existing yet
   b. fully developed
4. *inhibitions* (par. 4)
   a. shy feelings that stop you from acting naturally
   b. actions that show people how you feel
5. *willing* (par. 5)
   a. ready to do something
   b. not ready to do something
6. *impress* (par. 5)
   a. make people buy something
   b. make people understand something

C Organizing Information into an Outline

Organizing the information in a text can help you see it in a new way and improve your understanding of the text. One way to do this is to organize the information into an outline.

Complete the outline of the information in the reading. Use the six items below.

Can include telling jokes
Seeing the funny side of things
Laughter
Positive for the body
Controlled by brain and central nervous system
Developed over a lifetime

I. *Introduction: Sense of humor and laughter are important*

II. *Sense of humor*

A. ______

B. ______

C. ______

III. ______

A. ______

B. ______

D Relating Reading to Personal Experience

Discuss these questions with your classmates.

1. Do you think that you have a good sense of humor? Why or why not?
2. Do you understand the joke in paragraph 5? If so, explain it.
3. What is your favorite joke? Tell it.

Envy: Is It Hurting or Helping You?

Predicting

Look at the picture and the title of the reading. Then check (✓) the information that you think you will read about. Compare your answers with a partner.

_____ 1. a definition of envy

_____ 2. stories about people who have felt envy

_____ 3. stories about people who have never felt envy

_____ 4. reasons people feel envy

_____ 5. advice on how to deal with envy

_____ 6. results of a survey that asked people about envy

Skimming

Skim the reading to find which topics are and are not in the reading. Then read the whole text.

“Sometimes I'm so envious of my friends, I hate them,” says Kimberly. “I was at dinner a month ago, celebrating a friend's engagement. Suddenly I blurted out that 50 percent of marriages end in divorce. I was frustrated about not having a serious relationship myself. My envy took over, and I became a different person.” 1

2 Envy is the desire for what someone else has and resentment of that person for having it. Kimberley was envious, but that doesn't mean she is a bad person. "Everyone experiences envy – it's a normal human emotion," explains psychologist Karen Peterson.

3 Envy doesn't have to make us feel powerless and sorry for ourselves. Instead, it can motivate us to try to achieve what we want. There are effective ways for dealing with envy and turning it into something useful.

4 Kimberly's envy caused her to make the unkind remark about divorce. If you have a similar desire to express your envy in a negative way, stop yourself. Instead, think about what it is you're envious of. Kimberly admitted that when her friend announced her engagement, "it made me feel lonely and insecure." Once you figure out why you're envious, it's much easier to eventually grow from the experience. "Envy can be an excellent teacher," states Peterson, "as long as you are open to learning its lessons."

5 Lucy and her friend were both trying to get a better job at their company. Lucy thought that she would get the promotion, but things didn't work out that way. Instead, her friend got the job, and Lucy became upset and jealous. Full of envy, she started saying hurtful things about her friend. "That wasn't like me, but I couldn't think straight," she explains. Lucy said unkind things because not getting the job made her feel bad about herself, explains Peterson. Her reaction didn't make her feel better, though. It just strengthened her negative feelings. If something similar happens to you, Peterson says that you should try to understand why your friend got the promotion. That way you can learn from the experience instead of reacting in a negative way.

6 If you feel that getting what you want – marriage, a better job, lots of money – is impossible, remember that every big goal is made up of thousands of tiny steps. "Think of one or two small things that you could do each week to help you come closer to your ultimate goal. Then do them," advises Doreen Virtue, author of the book *I'd Change My Life If I Had More Time.*

7 Kimberley left her friend's party feeling guilty. She knew her behavior was wrong. But shortly after, she decided to make some changes that would improve her social life. That decision was the first step in developing a positive attitude and getting rid of her envy.

Adapted from *Cosmopolitan*

A Comprehension Check

These statements are false. Change one word in each statement to make it true.

1. The emotion of envy is ~~unusual~~ normal in humans.
2. Envy is something that some people feel.
3. Envy can teach you a lot about others.
4. Envy makes you feel good about yourself.
5. When you feel envy, try asking yourself where you are feeling it.
6. If you want to avoid feeling envy, set goals that seem impossible to achieve.

B Vocabulary Study

Find the words and phrases in *italics* in the reading. Are the meanings of the words and phrases in each pair similar or different? Write *S* (similar) or *D* (different).

____ 1. *envious* (par. 1) / *jealous* (par. 5)

____ 2. *blurted out* (par. 1) / *said* (par. 5)

____ 3. *engagement* (par. 1) / *divorce* (par. 1)

____ 4. *resentment* (par. 2) / *reaction* (par. 5)

____ 5. *figure out* (par. 4) / *understand* (par. 5)

____ 6. *insecure* (par. 4) / *upset* (par. 5)

____ 7. *think straight* (par. 5) / *remember* (par. 6)

____ 8. *lonely* (par. 4) / *guilty* (par. 7)

C Making Inferences

> **Sometimes the reader must infer, or figure out, what the writer did not explain or state directly in a text.**

Which person in the reading could have said each of the following statements? Write *Kimberly*, *Lucy*, *Doreen*, or *Karen*.

"I expected to get the better job."

1. ____________

"I wish I were engaged."

2. ____________

"My friend isn't a better worker than I am."

3. ____________

"If you envy someone, make some changes in your life."

4. ____________

"I get envious at times, just like everyone else."

5. ____________

"My friends have a better social life than I do."

6. ____________

D Relating Reading to Personal Experience

Discuss these questions with your classmates.

1. What advice would you give to someone who is envious of a friend who: a. gets a promotion at work? b. always looks good? c. gets invited to a lot of parties?
2. Have you ever had an experience that showed you how envy could be "an excellent teacher"? Explain your answer.
3. Do you think that this statement from the reading is true: "Everyone experiences envy – it's a normal human emotion."? Why or why not?

The Value of Tears

Thinking About What You Know

How much do you know about crying? Mark each statement *T* (true) or *F* (false). Compare your answers with a partner.

_____ 1. Crying is good for people's eyes and their health.

_____ 2. Crying relieves stress.

_____ 3. Only sad things make people cry.

_____ 4. Too much stress can make it difficult for people to cry.

_____ 5. Tears are a natural way for people to release their emotions.

Skimming

Skim the reading to check your answers. Then read the whole text.

1 Tears can ruin make-up, bring conversation to a stop, and give you a runny nose. They can leave you embarrassed and without energy. However, crying is a fact of life, and tears are very useful. Even when you're not crying, your eyes produce tears. These create a film[1] over the eye's surface. This film contains a substance that protects your eyes against infection.

[1] ***film:*** a thin layer of something

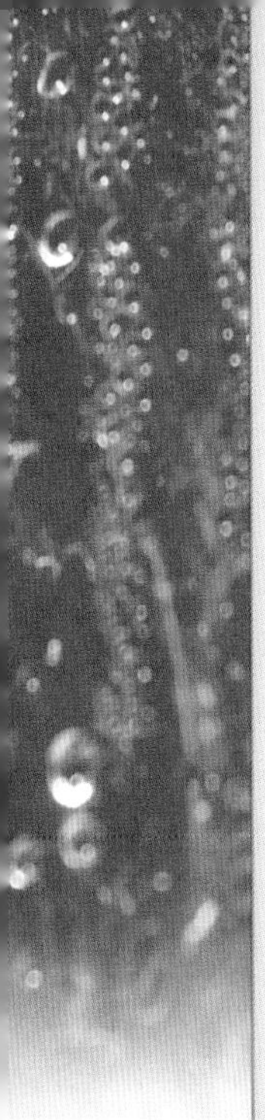

2 Tears relieve stress, but we tend to fight them for all sorts of reasons. "People worry about showing their emotions. They're afraid that once they lose control, they'll never get it back," explains psychologist Dorothy Rowe. "As children we were sometimes punished for shedding tears or expressing anger. As adults we still fear the consequences of showing emotions."

3 Almost any emotion – good or bad, happy or sad – can cause tears. Crying is a way that we release built-up emotions. Tears help you when you feel you are ready to explode because of very strong feelings. It may explain why people who are afraid to cry often suffer more heart attacks than people who cry more freely.

4 When some people become very stressed, however, they can't cry. They may be feeling shock, anger, fear, or grief, but they repress the emotion. "Everyone has the need to cry," says psychotherapist Vera Diamond. Sometimes in therapy sessions, patients participate in crying exercises. They practice crying so that they can get used to expressing emotion. Diamond says it's best to cry in safe, private places, like under the bedcovers or in the car. That's because many people get uncomfortable when others cry in front of them. In fact, they may be repressing their own need to cry.

5 In certain situations, such as at work, tears are not appropriate. It's good to hold back tears during a tense business discussion. "But once you are safely behind closed doors, don't just cry," Diamond says. She suggests that you act out the whole situation again and be as noisy and angry as you like. It will help you feel better. "And," she adds, "once your tears have released the stress, you can begin to think of logical ways to deal with the problem."

6 Tears are a sign of our ability to feel. You should never be afraid to cry.

Adapted from *Redbook*

A Comprehension Check

Every paragraph in the reading has one main idea. Write the correct paragraph number for each main idea.

_____ a. People's emotions cause them to cry.

_____ b. Crying has good effects on the body.

_____ c. There are times when it is better not to show your emotion immediately, but you should show it later.

_____ d. Crying is natural and shows that we have emotions.

_____ e. There are reasons why people don't like to cry.

_____ f. There are some helpful things that people can do if it is difficult for them to cry.

B Vocabulary Study

Find the words in the box in the reading. Then complete the sentences.

shedding (par. 2)	built-up (par. 3)	explode (par. 3)
grief (par. 4)	repress (par. 4)	tense (par. 5)

1. The situation was very ________________. I was worried and a little angry.
2. ________________ tears can make you feel better.
3. She was so angry that she felt like she was going to ________________.
4. You shouldn't ________________ your feelings. It's always good to express your emotions.
5. I felt such terrible ________________ when she died. I wanted to cry all the time.
6. His anger just kept growing until he had all this ________________ emotion.

C Recognizing Cause and Effect

When you read, it is important to recognize the reason why something happens (the cause). It is also important to recognize what happens as a result (the effect).

Reread paragraphs 1 and 3. Read sentences *a–f* below. Then write the letter of each sentence in the correct box to complete the cause-and-effect charts below.

a. We cry.
b. Eyes produce tears.
c. We release the emotions.
d. We have built-up emotions.
e. Tears create a film over the eye's surface.
f. The film protects the eyes against infections.

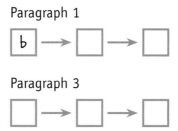

Paragraph 1

[b] → [ ] → [ ]

Paragraph 3

[ ] → [ ] → [ ]

D Relating Reading to Personal Experience

Discuss these questions with your classmates.

1. Are you uncomfortable when someone around you cries? What do you usually do when that happens?
2. In your experience, who cries more often, men or women? Why do you think that is true?
3. Do you think that people who can't cry should see a therapist? Why or why not?

Reread one of the unit readings and time yourself. Note your reading speed in the chart on page 124.

UNIT 11

Food

Look at the titles of the readings and their brief descriptions to preview this unit's content. Before you begin each reading, answer the questions about it.

Reading 1

Chocolate

Do you know how to tell the quality of chocolate? Do you believe that chocolate is bad for you? You can learn the truth about this popular treat in this excerpt from a reference book.

1. Do you like chocolate? How often do you eat it? How much do you eat at one time?
2. Is chocolate good or bad for you? Explain your answer.
3. What are three words that could describe chocolate?

Reading 2

Urban Farms

People who live in cities usually buy food that comes from far away, but today this is changing. This article discusses city people who are growing their own food locally.

1. Would you like to be a farmer? Why or why not?
2. Do you grow your own vegetables? If not, would you like to?
3. What are the advantages of eating locally grown vegetables?

Reading 3

It Tastes Just Like Chicken

Imagine that you have been invited to dinner in a foreign country. Your host puts a plate of strange-looking food in front of you. What should you do? This excerpt from a book offers some advice.

1. What are the most popular dishes in your culture? Do people normally eat these things in other cultures?
2. What are some types of food that you like? What don't you like?
3. If someone offers you food that you don't like, is it rude to refuse it? Why or why not?

Chocolate

Thinking About What You Know

How much do you know about chocolate? Mark each statement *T* (true) or *F* (false). Compare your answers with a partner.

_____ 1. Chocolate causes skin problems.

_____ 2. Chocolate should look smooth and shiny.

_____ 3. Chocolate is bad for the teeth.

_____ 4. Chocolate causes bad headaches.

_____ 5. Chocolate should start to melt when you hold it in your hand.

_____ 6. Chocolate causes weight problems.

Skimming

Skim the reading to check your answers. Then read the whole text.

Judging quality

1 We use all our senses – sight, smell, sound, touch, and taste – when we judge the quality of chocolate.

Sight: The chocolate should look smooth, very shiny, and dark brown in color.

Smell: The chocolate should not smell too sweet.

Sound: You should hear a clear "snap" when you break the chocolate in two.

Touch: Chocolate should start to melt when you hold it in your hand. In the mouth, it should feel very smooth, and it should melt immediately.

Taste: Chocolate contains many different flavors and aromas. The basic flavors are bitter, with a little acid taste, and sweet, with a little sour taste. There is also a tiny taste of salt, which makes the aromas of cocoa, pineapple, banana, vanilla, and cinnamon stronger.

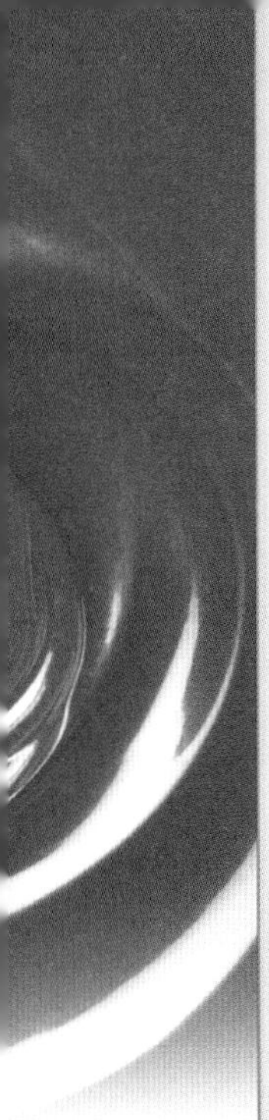

Tasting techniques

It is best to taste chocolate when you haven't eaten for a while. It is also best to eat it 2
at room temperature.

Allow the chocolate to sit in your mouth for a few moments to taste its basic flavors 3
and smell its aromas. Then chew it five to ten times to experience its other flavors and aromas. Let it gently touch the top of your mouth to get the full range of flavors. Finally, enjoy the tastes that stay in your mouth after you have swallowed the chocolate.

Common myths

You sometimes hear people say that chocolate is bad for your health. They usually are 4
talking about poor quality chocolate because it contains a lot of sugar and vegetable fat. However, good quality chocolate contains pure cacao butter with no added fat and very little sugar. Several doctors say that chocolate does not cause problems such as migraines, weight problems, acne, or tooth decay.

Migraines: Some people believe that chocolate contains large amounts of a chemical called tyramine. This chemical can cause migraines, or bad headaches. In fact, chocolate contains only a small amount of tyramine, much less than cheese does.

Weight problems: Good quality chocolate should not cause people to become overweight because it contains much less sugar than poor quality chocolate. And because good chocolate is more expensive, people don't usually eat large amounts of it.

Acne: Research does not show a connection between chocolate and skin problems, such as acne. Teenagers' acne is usually caused by changes in their bodies and also by their need for more fresh fruit and vegetables.

Tooth decay: Chocolate melts in the mouth and is in contact with the teeth only for a short time. Therefore, it does not damage the teeth as much as sticky candy.

Adapted from *The Cook's Encyclopedia of Chocolate*

A Comprehension Check

Read the statements about the people. Which part of the text should each person read? Write the correct letter.

_____ 1. Monica loves chocolate. However, she stopped eating it because she thinks it's bad for her.

_____ 2. Ahmed wants to learn how to appreciate chocolate more when he eats it.

_____ 3. Lin has five different kinds of chocolate and wants to know which is the best.

_____ 4. Celine took a bar of chocolate out of the refrigerator and ate it, but it didn't taste good.

_____ 5. Roberto wants to lose ten pounds, and he thinks he should stop eating chocolate.

a. Judging quality

b. Tasting techniques

c. Common myths

B Vocabulary Study

Cross out the word in each row that doesn't belong to the category in bold. If necessary, look back at the reading to see how the words are used.

1. **health problems**	acne	migraines	~~chemical~~	tooth decay
2. **how we judge chocolate**	color	aroma	flavor	amount
3. **kinds of taste**	bitter	sour	sticky	sweet
4. **what we do when we eat**	chew	melt	swallow	taste
5. **what chocolate contains**	sugar	fat	candy	cacao butter

C Identifying Supporting Details

Supporting details in a text explain the main ideas more fully. If you can identify supporting details, you will have a clearer understanding of the writer's ideas.

Look back at the reading and find the details to support these three main ideas.

1. There are several ways to identify good quality chocolate.
   a. the way it should look: ________________ and ________________
   b. the way it should smell: ________________________________
2. It's useful to know the best ways to taste chocolate.
   a. when you should taste it: ________________________________
   b. what you should try to taste and smell: ________________ and ________________
3. Some people are wrong about the effect of chocolate on health.
   three problems that chocolate does not cause: ________________,
   ________________, and ________________

D Relating Reading to Personal Experience

Discuss these questions with your classmates.

1. Why do you think so many people like chocolate?
2. What foods or drinks may cause migraines, weight problems, acne, or tooth decay?
3. Think of something you like to eat or drink. How do you judge its quality?.

Urban Farms

Previewing Vocabulary

These words and phrases are from the reading about urban farms. Discuss their meanings with a partner. Look up any new words in a dictionary. Mark each word or phrase *F* if it is usually associated with farms or *C* if it is usually associated with cities.

____ balconies	____ beehives	____ chemical fertilizers
____ crops	____ hens	____ parking lots
____ rooftops	____ seeds	____ spacious fields

Scanning

Scan the reading to find and circle the words and phrases that the writer uses to describe urban farms.

Normally when we think of a farm, we imagine quiet, spacious fields in the country, far away from the city. However, as cities around the world continue to grow, many of their residents are getting involved in urban agriculture. Today, small city farms are becoming more and more common. 1

Urban farming has important advantages for city people. First, it's good for the environment. The crops reduce the amount of carbon dioxide (CO_2) and increase the oxygen (O_2) in the air. As a result, they help clean the air. Second, locally grown food is fresher. It doesn't have to travel long distances, so it is less expensive, too. Urban residents also benefit from the enjoyment of farming. It can reduce the stress of city life. 2

3 Cuba is an example of a place that has had great success with city farming. Agriculture in Cuba used to depend on oil to drive tractors and other machinery that are needed on large farms. When oil got very expensive, Cuba started to create urban agriculture. The small farms of the city produce food crops without heavy equipment. The farmers don't use chemical fertilizers, either, so the food they grow is healthier. Today, the capital city Havana (with a population of about 2 million) has about 200 city farms. They grow crops such as lettuce, tomatoes, peppers, sweet potatoes, spinach, and herbs. This food is then sold at low prices in local markets.

4 China is another example. The Chinese government is encouraging people to start mini-farms on their balconies and in their yards. They can get free seeds and tools to help them. Many people are enjoying the experience. As one city farmer said, "Things that you grow yourself are extra tasty."

5 Some cities in the United States have tried another way of farming: edible walls. These walls have metal panels that are filled with soil and seeds. Edible walls can be used in small yards, parking lots, and many other places where there is not much space. They can produce fruit, vegetables, and herbs in far less space than it takes in a typical garden.

6 In Vancouver, Canada, a group of people used two blocks of empty yards for an urban garden. Neighbors worked on weekends to plant fruit and vegetables. Over time, they learned a lot about farming. Now they are also raising hens and setting up beehives for honey.

7 Community cooperation has been an important part of the success of urban farming projects in many parts of the world. Because of this cooperation, thousands of acres of rooftops, parking lots, walls, and yards are now helping to feed the cities' people.

A Comprehension Check

Complete the sentences with information from the reading.

1. An urban farm is a farm in the ________________.
2. Four countries with urban farms are ________________, ________________, ________________, ________________.
3. City farmers grow things on ________________ and in ________________.
4. People can get ________________ and ________________ from the Chinese government.
5. People grow food on walls when they don't have much ________________.
6. Because of urban farming, there is more ________________ for people who live in cities.

B Vocabulary Study

Find the words or phrases in the reading that match these definitions. The number of blanks represents the number of words in the answer.

1. interested in an activity and doing it ____________ (par. 1)
2. can be eaten ____________ (par. 5)
3. the material that plants grow in ____________ (par. 5)
4. areas with buildings surrounded by four streets ____________ (par. 6)
5. creating or putting something in place ________ ________ (par. 6)
6. measurements of land ____________ (par. 7)

C Recognizing Cause and Effect

> **When you read, it is important to recognize the reason why something happens (the cause). It is also important to recognize what happens as a result (the effect).**

Match each cause to its effect according to the reading.

CAUSE	EFFECT
____ 1. Oil got very expensive.	a. The food is fresher and less expensive.
____ 2. The crops reduce the amount of carbon dioxide and increase the oxygen.	b. Cuba started to create urban agriculture.
____ 3. Locally grown food doesn't have to travel long distances.	c. Some cities have tried edible walls.
____ 4. Urban residents also benefit from the enjoyment of farming.	d. They help clean the air.
____ 5. The farmers don't use chemical fertilizers.	e. It can reduce the stress of city life.
____ 6. There is not much space for farming in U.S. cities.	f. The food is healthier.

D Relating Reading to Personal Experience

Discuss these questions with your classmates.

1. Would you like to get involved in urban farming? Why or why not?
2. Is urban farming a good idea for your town? If not, why not? If so, where in your town is a good place for an urban farm?
3. What problems could urban farming cause?

Reading 3

It Tastes Just Like Chicken

Thinking About the Topic

Read the list of foods in the chart. Look up any new words in a dictionary. Then check (✓) the columns that are true for you. Compare your answers with a partner.

	I never eat this.	I sometimes eat this.	I often eat this.
apple pie			
chicken			
lobster			
oysters			
rat			
roasted ants			
sheep's eyeballs			
snake			
steak			

Scanning

Scan the reading to find and circle the names of food that people in the United States, Saudi Arabia, and Colombia eat. Then read the whole text.

1 When you are away from home, eating is more than just a way to keep your stomach full. Sharing a meal with others is a kind of communication. There is no better way to say, "Glad to meet you . . . glad to be doing business with you . . . ."

2 Clearly, mealtime is not the time for you to say "Thanks, but no thanks." When you are in a foreign country, saying yes to the food on your plate is important. It means that you accept the host, the country, and the company. That's why most experienced travelers try to eat everything everywhere, even if the dish looks strange.

3 What would people in the United States think of a visitor who didn't want to try a bite of homemade apple pie or a sizzling steak? What would they think of a guest who didn't want to taste an oyster or a lobster? A lobster, for example, may remind people of something from a science fiction movie, not something you eat with melted butter. We often feel uncomfortable with food that we are unfamiliar with. However, food that seems

strange in one culture may be a favorite food in another. For instance, sheep's eyeballs may be unfamiliar in some parts of the world, but in Saudi Arabia, they are a delicacy. In parts of Colombia, roasted ants are.

Can you refuse such food without being rude? Most experienced business travelers say no. You should at least take a few bites. It helps, though, to cut things into very thin slices. This way, you won't notice the texture or remember where it came from. Or, "Swallow it quickly," as one traveler recommends. "I still can't tell you what roasted ants taste like." And when you are wondering about the taste, "it tastes just like chicken" is often thankfully true. Even when the "it" is really rat or snake. 4

Another useful piece of advice is this: It's better if you don't know what you are eating. Don't ask what's for dinner. Avoid glancing into the kitchen or looking at restaurant menus. Your host will be very happy because you are eating the food that he or she offers. And who knows? Maybe it really is chicken in that stew. 5

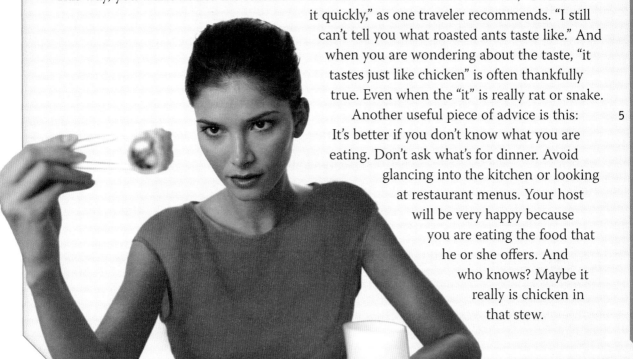

Adapted from *The Do's and Taboos of Body Language Around the World*

A Comprehension Check

For each question, two of the answers are correct. Cross out the answer that is *not* correct.

1. In a foreign country, why is it important to eat the food people offer you?
   a. It is polite.
   b. It is important to know what people eat in other countries.
   c. It is a form of communication.
2. What usually bothers people about certain kinds of food?
   a. the way it looks
   b. the way it feels in the mouth
   c. the way it is cooked
3. What types of food might visitors to the United States find strange?
   a. lobsters
   b. oysters
   c. chicken
4. What should you do when someone offers you food that you do not know or like?
   a. Ask what you are eating.
   b. Cut the food into very small pieces.
   c. Swallow it quickly.

B Vocabulary Study

Find the words in the box in the reading. Then complete the sentences.

host (par. 2 & 5)	dish (par. 2)	delicacy (par. 3)
slices (par. 4)	texture (par. 4)	stew (par. 5)

1. This ice cream has a very smooth ________________.
2. His favorite ________________ is roast chicken.
3. ________________ is made from meat and vegetables cooked in a little sauce.
4. If you are invited to someone's home, bring flowers to the ________________.
5. She's going to cut the meat now. How many ________________ do you want?
6. A ________________ is something that people don't eat often because it's expensive.

C Recognizing Purpose

Writers create texts for different purposes. For example, sometimes a writer wants to give information. Other times, the writer wants to influence the reader's thinking in some way. Recognizing a writer's purpose will help you better understand what you read.

Check (✓) the writer's main purpose in the reading.

____ 1. to tell a story

____ 2. to give information about food in different countries

____ 3. to give advice

____ 4. to persuade people to travel

D Relating Reading to Personal Experience

Discuss these questions with your classmates.

1. Which kinds of food in the reading would you *not* want to eat? What would you do if someone offered you the food?
2. What kinds of food do you consider delicacies? Why?
3. What food in your culture might a visitor find strange?

Reread one of the unit readings and time yourself. Note your reading speed in the chart on page 124.

UNIT 12 Sleep and Dreams

Look at the titles of the readings and their brief descriptions to preview this unit's content. Before you begin each reading, answer the questions about it.

Reading 1

Power Napping Is Good for the I.Q.

Do you find that you can't think clearly when you don't get enough sleep? This newspaper article reviews research on the connection between sleep and intelligence.

1. How much sleep do you usually get? When do you usually go to bed? When do you usually wake up?
2. How much sleep do you think people need to be able to function well during the day?
3. Do you ever take naps? If so, how long do you usually sleep? Are you in a better mood after a nap?

Reading 2

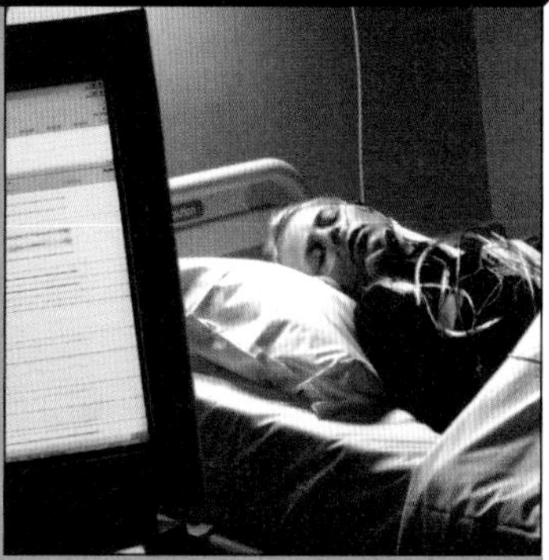

Common Questions About Dreams

This article from the Internet answers some questions that people frequently ask about dreams.

1. Do you think everyone dreams? Why or why not?
2. Have you had a vivid or powerful dream recently? If so, describe it.
3. What are some questions that you would like to ask an expert on dreams?

Reading 3

What Is a Dream?

In this newspaper article, learn about different theories on the meaning of dreams.

1. Do you think that dreams are important? Why or why not?
2. Have you ever noticed a connection between your dreams and your everyday life? If so, give an example.
3. Do you think that dreams can tell you anything about the future? Why or why not?

Power Napping Is Good for the I.Q.

Predicting

Look at the title of the reading and the definition of *I.Q.* at the end of the reading on page 113. Then check (✓) the statement that you think will be the main idea of the text. Compare your answer with a partner.

_____ 1. The amount of sleep that you get affects how well your brain functions.

_____ 2. You should sleep before you take an intelligence test.

_____ 3. People in power are more intelligent because they take naps.

_____ 4. It is possible to know if a person gets enough sleep by testing the brain.

Skimming

Skim the reading to check your prediction. Then read the whole text.

1 Today we hear more and more about the importance of getting enough sleep – about eight hours a night. Sleep can help heal and give energy to both the body and the brain. Medical experts now believe that sleep is even more important for health than diet or exercise. It seems almost certain that the third of our lives that we spend asleep has a great effect on the two-thirds that we are awake. Sleep affects our emotions, memory, focus, and behavior.

Studies show that people in developed countries spend less time asleep and more time at work or commuting. Dr. Karine Spiegel, at the University of Chicago, has found that the average length of sleep has gone down from nine hours a night in 1910 to seven-and-a-half hours a night today. However, our bodies cannot function well without enough sleep. Losing just one or two hours of sleep a night, over a long period of time, can cause serious health problems. 2

According to Canadian scientist Dr. Stanley Coren, every hour of lost sleep at night causes us to lose one I.Q.[1] point the next day. For example, when someone gets only five or six hours of sleep each night for a week, the person's I.Q. could go down 15 points or more. That's why, without enough sleep, a normally intelligent person may start to have difficulty doing daily tasks. 3

Most sleep experts say that humans need at least eight hours of sleep every day, but it should be in two stages: a long sleep at night and a shorter nap in the afternoon. Some companies help their employees follow this advice. They allow them to "power nap" in the afternoon, if only for 20 minutes. They say this makes the workers much more efficient. 4

To study sleep deprivation (not getting enough sleep), scientists use a test called the Multiple Sleep Latency Test (MSLT). During the test, a person stays in a darkened, quiet room during the daytime. Scientists believe that a sleep-deprived person will fall asleep quickly. If it takes ten minutes or longer to fall asleep, the person is probably getting enough sleep. 5

Scientists have also found that the time of year seems to affect how much sleep we need. People usually sleep longer in the winter, sometimes as much as 14 hours a night. However, in the summer, people sometimes sleep as little as six hours, without having any problems. 6

---

[1] ***I.Q. (intelligence quotient):*** a person's level of intelligence that is measured by certain tests

Adapted from *The Scotsman*

A Comprehension Check

Answer the following questions with a partner.

1. What do medical experts say about sleep? (par. 1)
2. Do people sleep more or less nowadays than they slept in the past? (par. 2)
3. According to Dr. Coren, what will happen to a person's I.Q. if he or she loses an hour of sleep at night? (par. 3)
4. How many hours of sleep do experts tell us to get? What's the best way to get this sleep? (par. 1 & 4)
5. What happens to employees who take a short nap at work? (par. 4)
6. How much sleep do people need at different times of the year? (par. 6)

B Vocabulary Study

Find the words in *italics* in the reading. Then match each word with its meaning.

____ 1. *diet* (par. 1)	a. complete attention
____ 2. *focus* (par. 1)	b. working well, without wasting time
____ 3. *commuting* (par. 2)	c. work to be done
____ 4. *tasks* (par. 3)	d. traveling regularly between work and home
____ 5 *stages* (par. 4)	e. what people usually eat and drink
____ 6. *efficient* (par. 4)	f. parts of an activity

C Summarizing

When you summarize a text, you include only the most important information. A summary does not include details or examples. Summarizing is a strategy that can help you check your understanding of a text.

Choose six of the words below to complete the summary of the reading.

better	diet	eight	employees	less	managers
more	naps	six	sleep	tests	worse

_______________ (1) is very important for our health, but nowadays people are sleeping _______________ (2) than they used to. Scientists recommend that people sleep at least _______________ (3) hours every day, but not all at one time. Because scientists have found that sleep helps people do their daily tasks _______________ (4), some companies allow _______________ (5) to take _______________ (6) at work.

D Relating Reading to Personal Experience

Discuss these questions with your classmates.

1. When you don't get enough sleep, does it affect your efficiency at school or at work? If so, how?
2. Will you change your sleeping habits after reading this article? Why or why not?
3. What is your ideal sleeping schedule? Do you usually follow it? Why or why not?

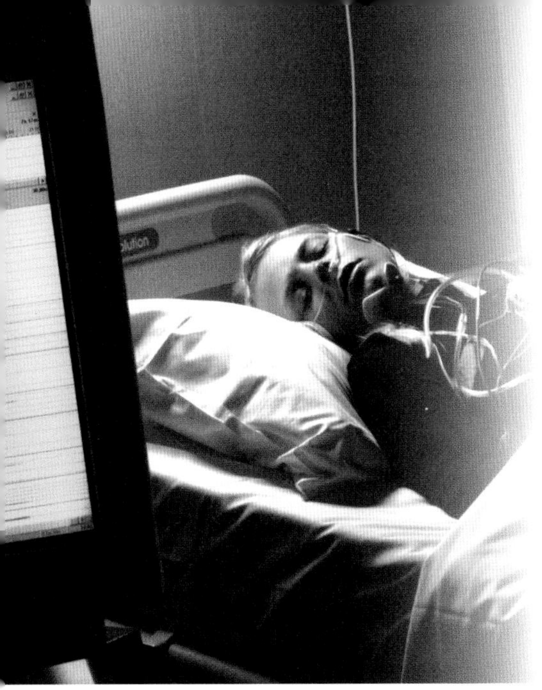

Common Questions About Dreams

Thinking About What You Know

How much do you know about your dreams? Check (✓) *yes* or *no*. Compare your answers with a partner.

	Yes	No
1. Do you have dreams?		
2. Do you usually remember your dreams?		
3. Are your dreams in color?		
4. Do you think your dreams have meaning?		
5. Do you understand your dreams?		

Skimming

Skim the reading. Compare your answers to what experts say about dreams. Then read the whole text.

Does everyone dream?

1 Yes. Research shows that we all dream. We have our most vivid dreams during a type of sleep called Rapid Eye Movement (REM) sleep. During REM sleep, the brain is very active. The eyes move quickly back and forth under the lids, and the large muscles of the body are relaxed. REM sleep occurs every 90–100 minutes, three to four times a night, and it lasts longer as the night goes on. The final REM period may last as long as 45 minutes. We dream at other times during the night, too, but those dreams are less vivid.

Do people remember their dreams?

2 A few people remember their dreams. However, most people forget nearly everything that happened during the night – dreams, thoughts, and the short periods of time when

they were awake. Sometimes, though, people suddenly remember a dream later in the day or on another day. It seems that the memory of the dream is not totally lost, but for some reason it is very hard to bring it back. If you want to remember your dream, the best thing to do is to write it down as soon as you wake up.

Are dreams in color?

3 Most dreams are in color. However, people may not be aware of it for two reasons: They don't usually remember the details of their dreams, or they don't notice the color because it is such a natural part of our lives. People who are very aware of color when they are awake probably notice color more often in their dreams.

Do dreams have meaning?

4 Scientists continue to debate this issue. However, people who spend time thinking about their dreams believe that they are meaningful and useful. Some people use dreams to help them learn more about their feelings, thoughts, behavior, motives, and values. Others find that dreams can help them solve problems. It's also true that artists, writers, and scientists often get creative ideas from dreams.

How can I learn to understand my dreams?

5 The most important thing to remember is that your dreams are personal. The people, actions, and situations in your dreams reflect your experience, your thoughts, and your feelings. Some dream experts believe that there are certain types of dreams that many people have, even if they come from different cultures or time periods. Usually, however, the same dream will have different meanings for different people. For example, an elephant in a dream may mean one thing to a zookeeper and something very different to a child whose favorite toy is a stuffed elephant. To learn to understand your dreams, think about what each part of the dream means to you or reminds you of. Then look for links between your dreams and what is happening in your daily life. If you think hard and you are patient, perhaps the meaning of your dreams will become clearer to you.

Adapted from www.asdreams.org

A Comprehension Check

For each question, two of the answers are correct. Cross out the answer that is *not* correct.

1. What do we know about REM sleep?
   a. It happens more than once a night.
   b. It is during REM sleep that people experience all their dreams.
   c. Except for the final REM period, REM sleep usually lasts less than 45 minutes.
2. How can remembering dreams be helpful?
   a. The dreamer may be able to understand his or her feelings better.
   b. The dreamer may get useful ideas in his or her dreams.
   c. The dreamer may be able to predict the future.
3. What do we know about the meaning of dreams?
   a. It is possible to learn to understand your dreams.
   b. A dream about a car will mean the same thing to you and a friend.
   c. There are connections between your dreams and your daily life.

B Vocabulary Study

Find the words in the box in the reading. Then complete the sentences.

last (par. 1)	issue (par. 4)	motives (par. 4)
values (par. 4)	reflect (par. 5)	patient (par. 5)

1. Her dreams about flying ______________ her wish to escape.
2. Some dreams ______________ as long as 30 minutes or more.
3. At the town meeting, they discussed the ______________ of raising taxes.
4. It takes years to learn another language. You have to be ______________.
5. He needed money. Can you think of any other ______________ for the robbery?
6. People with the right ______________ know the difference between right and wrong.

C Thinking Beyond the Text

Good readers are able to go beyond the words that a writer actually uses and understand ideas that the writer never directly expresses. One way to practice this strategy is to imagine other information that the writer could have added about the topic.

Read the statements in the chart. If these statements were added to the reading, which paragraph would they each fit into? Check (✓) the correct paragraph.

	Par. 1	Par. 2	Par. 3	Par. 4	Par. 5
1. That's why some people think their dreams are black and white.					
2. Dreams can help people understand themselves better.					
3. If you wish, you can find books that can help you understand your dreams.					
4. If you can't remember your whole dream, write down the last part you remember.					
5. Our most powerful dreams don't happen during deep sleep.					

D Relating Reading to Personal Experience

Discuss these questions with your classmates.

1. Do you ever have the same dream again and again? Why do you think that happens?
2. Has a dream ever helped you solve a problem? If so, what was it?
3. Have you ever gotten a creative idea from a dream? If so, what was it?

What Is a Dream?

Thinking About the Topic

The words in the box are from the reading. Discuss the meanings of the words with a partner. Look up any new words in a dictionary.

crime	emotions	fears	heroes
mental skill	messages	panic	wishes

Scanning

Scan the reading to find and circle the words in the box. Then read the whole text.

1 For centuries, people have wondered about the strange things that they dream about. Some psychologists say that this nighttime activity of the mind has no special meaning. Others, however, think that dreams are an important part of our lives. In fact, many experts believe that dreams can tell us about a person's mind and emotions.

2 Before modern times, many people thought that dreams contained messages from God. It was only in the twentieth century that people started to study dreams in a scientific way.

3 The Austrian psychologist, Sigmund Freud, was probably the first person to study dreams scientifically. In his famous book, *The Interpretation of Dreams* (1900), Freud wrote that dreams are an expression of a person's wishes. He believed that dreams allow people to express the feelings, thoughts, and fears that they are afraid to express in real life.

The Swiss psychiatrist Carl Jung was once a student of Freud's. Jung, however, had a different idea about dreams. Jung believed that the purpose of a dream was to communicate a message to the dreamer. He thought people could learn more about themselves by thinking about their dreams. For example, people who dream about falling may learn that they have too high an opinion of themselves. On the other hand, people who dream about being heroes may learn that they think too little of themselves. 4

Modern-day psychologists continue to develop theories about dreams. For example, psychologist William Domhoff from the University of California, Santa Cruz, believes that dreams are tightly linked to a person's daily life, thoughts, and behavior. A criminal, for example, might dream about crime. 5

Domhoff believes that there is a connection between dreams and age. His research shows that children do not dream as much as adults. According to Domhoff, dreaming is a mental skill that needs time to develop. 6

He has also found a link between dreams and gender. His studies show that the dreams of men and women are different. For example, the people in men's dreams are often other men, and the dreams often involve fighting. This is not true of women's dreams. Domhoff found this gender difference in the dreams of people from 11 cultures around the world, including both modern and traditional ones. 7

Can dreams help us understand ourselves? Psychologists continue to try to answer this question in different ways. However, one thing they agree on is this: If you dream that something terrible is going to occur, you shouldn't panic. The dream may have meaning, but it does not mean that some terrible event will actually take place. It's important to remember that the world of dreams is not the real world. 8

Adapted from *The Straits Times*, Singapore

A Comprehension Check

Mark each statement *T* (true) or *F* (false). Then correct the false statements. The first one is marked for you.

__F__ 1. There were scientific studies of dreams in the ~~1800s~~ 1900s.

____ 2. Not everyone agrees that dreams are meaningful.

____ 3. According to Freud, people dream about things that they cannot talk about.

____ 4. Jung believed that the purpose of a dream was to communicate a message from God.

____ 5. Things that happen to you during the day can affect your dreams at night.

____ 6. According to Domhoff, babies do not have the same ability to dream as adults do.

____ 7. Men and women dream about different things.

____ 8. Scientists agree that dreams predict the future.

B Vocabulary Study

Find the words in the reading that match these definitions.

1. hundreds of years ________________ (par. 1)
2. thought about in a questioning way ________________ (par. 1)
3. closely ________________ (par. 5)
4. a connection ________________ (par. 7)
5. the male or female sex ________________ (par. 7)
6. happen ________________ (par. 8)

C Understanding Pronoun Reference

Writers use different kinds of pronouns to refer to information that is stated earlier in a text. Some common pronouns are *his, they, this,* and *one(s)*. Understanding pronoun reference is very important for reading comprehension.

What do the pronouns in italics refer to? Circle the letter of the correct answer.

1. *they* (par. 1, line 1)	a. people	b. things
2. *his* (par. 3, line 2)	a. Sigmund Freud's	b. Carl Jung's
3. *they* (par. 3, line 4)	a. fears	b. people
4. *they* (par. 4, line 6)	a. heroes	b. people who dream about being heroes
5. *This* (par. 7, line 3)	a. men's dreams	b. dreams that involve fighting
6. *ones* (par. 7, line 5)	a. cultures	b. gender differences

D Relating Reading to Personal Experience

Discuss these questions with your classmates.

1. What topics do you often dream about? Why do you think you dream about these things?
2. Would you like to learn to understand your dreams? Why or why not?
3. Take a poll. Ask your classmates *Which of the following things do you never dream about: nature, flying, friends, sports, money, school, or work?* Then discuss the results of the poll.

Reread one of the unit readings and time yourself. Note your reading speed in the chart on page 124.

Increasing Your Reading Speed

Good readers understand what they read, and they read at a good speed. Thus, for you to become a fluent reader in English, you need to improve your ability to understand what you are reading; you also need to improve your reading speed.

To do this, you should time yourself when you read a text that is not difficult for you. You may want to read a text several times before you time yourself, or you may want to read the text several times and time yourself after each reading. Both ways will help you improve your reading speed.

The chart on page 124 will help you keep a record of how your reading speed is improving.

After you have completed a unit, time yourself on at least one of the readings. Write down the time when you start reading the text. Then write down the time when you finish reading the text. Calculate the number of minutes and seconds it took you to read the text.

Use the chart below and on pages 122–123 to figure out your reading speed. Divide the number of words in a text by the amount of time it took you to read it. That is your reading speed. For example, if the text is 425 words long and it took you five minutes and 30 seconds to read the text, your reading speed is 77.27 words per minute ($425 \div 5.5 = 77.27$).

As you go through the book, the number of words you can read in a minute should go up. That means your reading fluency is getting better.

Unit	Title of Text	Number of Words in Text	Amount of Time to Read the Text	Reading Speed (wpm = words per minute)
Unit 1 **Culture**	Adventures in India	447 words	_____ minutes & _____ seconds	_______ wpm
	Body Language in the United States	444 words	_____ minutes & _____ seconds	_______ wpm
	Hot Spots in Cross-Cultural Communication	459 words	_____ minutes & _____ seconds	_______ wpm
Unit 2 **Money**	Shopaholics	351 words	_____ minutes & _____ seconds	_______ wpm
	Young Millionaires	417 words	_____ minutes & _____ seconds	_______ wpm
	Pity the Poor Lottery Winner	352 words	_____ minutes & _____ seconds	_______ wpm

Unit	Title of Text	Number of Words in Text	Amount of Time to Read the Text	Reading Speed (wpm = words per minute)
Unit 3 **Sports**	The Ancient Olympic Games	376 words	_____ minutes & _____ seconds	_______ wpm
	The Greatest Marathon Runner	393 words	_____ minutes & _____ seconds	_______ wpm
	Extreme Sports	518 words	_____ minutes & _____ seconds	_______ wpm
Unit 4 **Music**	Music and Moods	256 words	_____ minutes & _____ seconds	_______ wpm
	I'll Be Bach	388 words	_____ minutes & _____ seconds	_______ wpm
	The Biology of Music	422 words	_____ minutes & _____ seconds	_______ wpm
Unit 5 **Animals**	The Penguins of Brazil	376 words	_____ minutes & _____ seconds	_______ wpm
	Exotic Animals – Not as Pets!	371 words	_____ minutes & _____ seconds	_______ wpm
	Let's Abandon Zoos	362 words	_____ minutes & _____ seconds	_______ wpm
Unit 6 **Travel**	Vacationing in Space	403 words	_____ minutes & _____ seconds	_______ wpm
	Ecotourism	355 words	_____ minutes & _____ seconds	_______ wpm
	Jet Lag	352 words	_____ minutes & _____ seconds	_______ wpm
Unit 7 **The Internet**	Love on the Internet	436 words	_____ minutes & _____ seconds	_______ wpm
	Help on the Internet	452 words	_____ minutes & _____ seconds	_______ wpm
	How Wikis Work	406 words	_____ minutes & _____ seconds	_______ wpm

Unit	Title of Text	Number of Words in Text	Amount of Time to Read the Text	Reading Speed (wpm = words per minute)
Unit 8 **Friends**	Ten Easy Ways to Make Friends	428 words	_____ minutes & _____ seconds	________ wpm
	Best Friends	379 words	_____ minutes & _____ seconds	________ wpm
	Are Online Friends Real Friends?	424 words	_____ minutes & _____ seconds	________ wpm
Unit 9 **Gifts**	Gift Giving	420 words	_____ minutes & _____ seconds	________ wpm
	Modern Day Self-Sacrifice	340 words	_____ minutes & _____ seconds	________ wpm
	Gift Cards	431 words	_____ minutes & _____ seconds	________ wpm
Unit 10 **Emotions**	Do You Have a Sense of Humor?	345 words	_____ minutes & _____ seconds	________ wpm
	Envy: Is It Hurting or Helping You?	460 words	_____ minutes & _____ seconds	________ wpm
	The Value of Tears	370 words	_____ minutes & _____ seconds	________ wpm
Unit 11 **Food**	Chocolate	420 words	_____ minutes & _____ seconds	________ wpm
	Urban Farms	433 words	_____ minutes & _____ seconds	________ wpm
	It Tastes Just Like Chicken	375 words	_____ minutes & _____ seconds	________ wpm
Unit 12 **Sleep and Dreams**	Power Napping Is Good for the I.Q.	397 words	_____ minutes & _____ seconds	________ wpm
	Common Questions About Dreams	479 words	_____ minutes & _____ seconds	________ wpm
	What Is a Dream?	434 words	_____ minutes & _____ seconds	________ wpm

Reading Speed Progress Chart

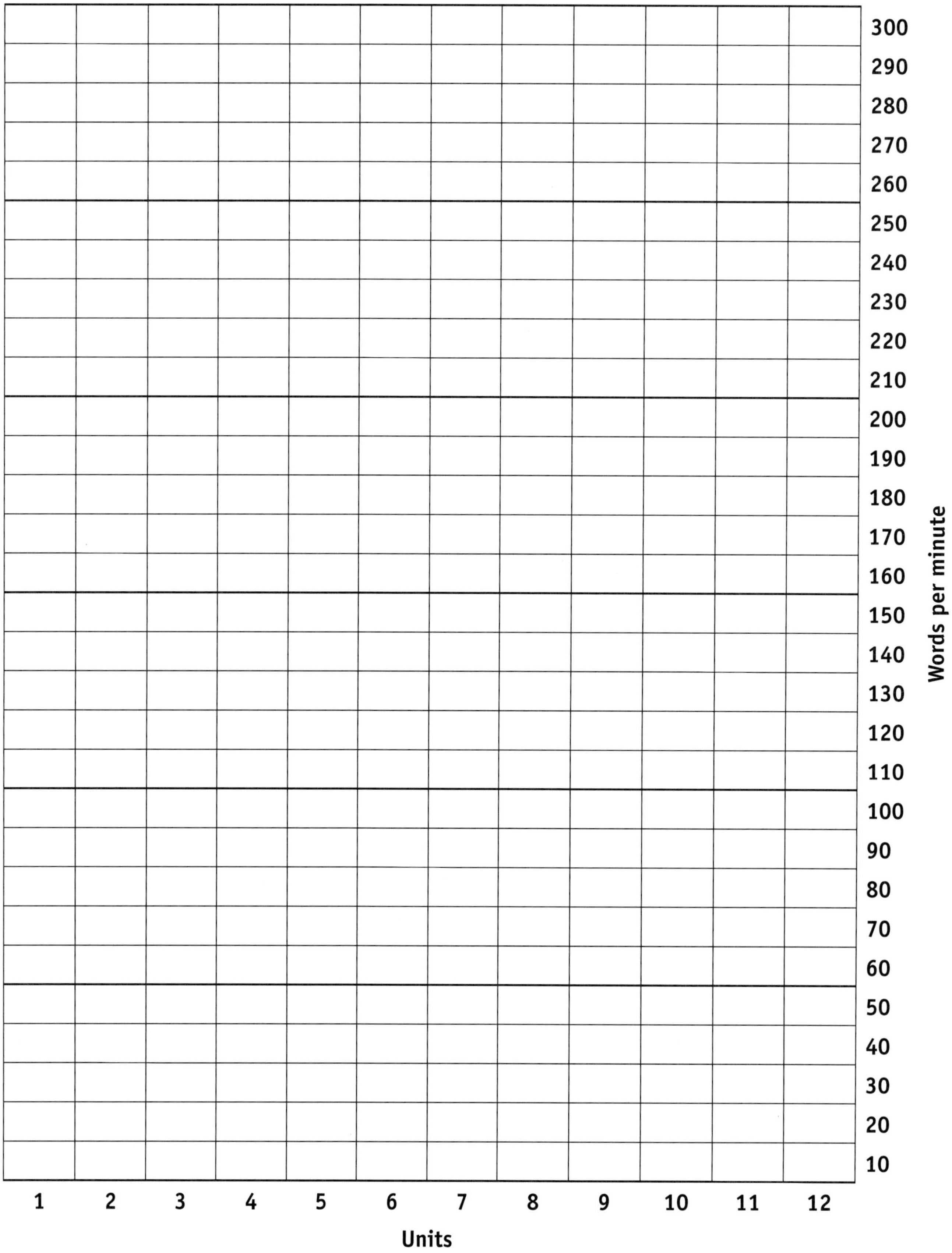

Text and Art Credits

The authors and publishers acknowledge use of the following sources and are grateful for the permissions granted. While every effort has been made, it has not always been possible to identify the sources of all the material used, or to trace all copyright holders. If any omissions are brought to our notice, we will be happy to include the appropriate acknowledgements on reprinting.

2–3 Adapted from www.climbtothestars.org/india/. Copyright © Stephanie Booth. http://climbtothestars.org/logbook. Reprinted with permission.

5–6 Adapted from *Gestures: the Do's and Taboos of Body Language around the World* by Roger E Axtell. Copyright © John Wiley & Sons, Inc. Reprinted with permission.

8–9 Adapted from "Tips for Successful Cross Cultural Communication" by A J Schuler http://www.SchulerSolutions.com. Dr A J Schuler is a speaker, consultant and leadership coach. To find out more about his programs and services visit www.AJSchuler.com.

12–13 Sources: http://money.cnn.com/2003/10/31/pf/shopaholics/; http://www.shopaholicsanonymous.org/checklist.htm.

15–16 Sources: http://money.msn.com/investing/how-to-be-a-millionaire-by-age-25-kiplinger.aspx; http://nichemarketingweb.net/08/14/young-millionaire-secrets/; http://ezinearticles.com/?Secrets-of-Young-Millionaires&id=1780198; http://www.entrepreneur.com/worklife/successstories/youngmillionaires/article196572.html.

19 Adapted from "Not a lotto luck. Pity the poor lottery winner" by Lois Gould. *New York Times Magazine.* Copyright © 1995 Star Tribune.

22–23 Adapted from "The Ancient Olympics exhibit" (www.perseus.tufts.edu/Olympics/). Courtesy of the Perseus Digital Library (www.perseus.tufts.edu). Accessed 01/04/2011.

25–26 Adapted from "The Greatest Marathon Runner" by Robert Key http://www.faithfulsoles.com/StoriesAll/00001-TheGreatestMarathoner.htm Reprinted with permission.

28–29 Sources: http://www.buzzle.com/articles/what-makes-people-do-extreme-sports.htmlhttp://adventure.howstuffworks.com/paragliding.htm/printable; http://www.wisegeek.com/what-is-the-difference-between-a-mountain-bike-and-a-road-bike.htm; http://www.essortment.com/hobbies/freeridingfreer_swcz.htm; http://www.smithsonianmag.com/history-archaeology/The-Top-Ten-Most-Important-Moments-in-Snowboarding-History.html?c=y&page=1.

33 Adapted from "Lift your spirits with Music" by Lisa Miller, *Woman's Day* 08/01/2000. Reprinted with permission of Hachette Filipacchi Media US Inc.

35–36 Adapted from "I'll be Bach" by Chris Wilson, *Slate Magazine*, 05/19/2010. All rights reserved. Used by permission and protected by the Copyright Laws of the United States. The printing, copying, redistribution or transmission of the Material without express written permission is prohibited.

38–39 Adapted from "The biology of music" *The Economist*, 02/10/2000. Reprinted with permission.

42–43 Adapted from "The Penguins of Brazil" by Edgard Telles Ribeiro, The New York Times 11/29/2009. Copyright © 2009 *The New York Times*. All rights reserved/ Used by permission and protected by the Copyright Laws of the United States. The printing, copying, redistribution or retransmission of this Content without express written permission is prohibited.

45–46 Adapted from "New York's Wild Kingdom: Lions and tigers and bears, oh my – all have been found in somebody's apartment" by Eric Sabo, *Newsday* 06/25/94.

48–49 Adapted from "For the animals' sake, let's abandon zoos" by Susan A Scholterer, *The Buffalo News*, 04/04/2000.

52–53 Sources: http://www.travelex.co.uk/press/ENG/DOC_QUID_10042007.asp; http://www.space.com/4454-scientists-design-space-currency.html; http://www.spacefuture.com/tourism/hotels.shtml.

55–56 Sources: http://www.piedrablanca.org/eco-project.htm; http://www.tripulu.com/2010/09/30/punta-laguna-quintana-roo-mexico-321; http://www.eco-tours.co.nz/; http://www.infohub.com/vacation_packages/5725.html; http://www.tourism.net.nz/new-zealand/nz/nature-and-eco-tourism/.

58–59 Adapted from *Overcoming Jet Lag* by Dr Charles F Ehret and Lynne Waller Scanlon, published by Berkeley Books, New York,1983.

62–63 Adapted from "Star-crossed Asian lovers click with net matchmaker" by Stephen Farrell, *The Times* (London), 03/30/2000. Reprinted with permission.

65–66 Adapted from "Cry for Help on the Internet" by Malcolm McConnell. Reprinted with permission from *The Reader's Digest*, October 1997. Copyright © 1997 by The Reader's Digest Association, Inc.

68–69 Sources: http://computer.howstuffworks.com/internet/basics/wiki.htm; http://www.makeuseof.com/tag/8-sister-wikis-from-wikipedia-we-should-be-aware-about/; http://www.educause.edu/ELI/7ThingsYouShouldKnowAboutWikis/156807.

72–73 Adapted from "10 easy ways to make friends" by Alison Bell, *Teen Magazine*, April 1994. Reprinted with permission of Alison Bell.

75–76 Adapted from the Introduction *Best Friends*. Published by Doubleday. Copyright © 1998 by Caroline Saline and Sharon Wohlmuth. Reprinted by permission of Caroline Saline and Sharon Wohlmuth.

78–79 Sources: http://arstechnica.com/old/content/2006/11/8326.ars; http://www.dnaindia.com/bangalore/report_in-digital-age-whats-friendships-status-message_1417173; http://hubpages.com/hub/Making-Friends-On-The-InternetbyDarkwing; http://momgrind.com/2008/06/20/the-blurry-line-between-online-and-real-life-friendships/; http://hubpages.com/hub/How-to-make-great-friends-through-social-networking-online-or-face-to-face; http://www.teachingvillage.org/2010/11/18/very-cool-meeting-online-friends-face-to-face/.

82–83 Adapted from *A Celebration of Customs & Rituals of the World* by Robert Ingpen and Philip Wilkinson, published by Facts on File, Inc. Copyright © 1994 by Facts on File, Inc., an imprint of Infobase Learning. Reprinted with permission by Facts on File, Inc., and Philip Wilkinson.

85–86 Adapted from "Modern Day Gift of the Magi" www.drlaura.com. Copyright, Take on the Day, LLC. Reprinted with permission.

88–89 Sources: http://articles.moneycentral.msn.com/SavingandDebt/FindDealsOnline/GiftCardsAreNotGifts.aspx?page=all; http://www.nytimes.com/2007/01/07/magazine/07wwln_freak.t.html.

92–93 Adapted from "Jokes can't always make you laugh" by Steve Wilson, www.laughterclubs.com. Reprinted with permission.

95–96 Adapted from "Envy: Is it hurting or (surprise) helping you?" by Julie Taylor, *Cosmopolitan* 03/01/1998.

98–99 Adapted from "Cheers for Tears" by Trudy Culross, *Redbook Magazine*, October 1994. Reprinted with permission.

102–103 Adapted from *The Cook's Encyclopedia of Chocolate* by Christine McFadden and Christine France, published by Barnes & Noble, 2000.

105–106 Sources: http://www.nytimes.com/2009/11/19/business/energy-environment/19WALLS.html?_r=1&ref=urban_agriculture; http://articles.cnn.com/2010-04-08/world/urban.farming.city.growing.food_1_special-period-havana-local-markets?_s=PM:WORLD; http://www.cityfarmer.info/?s=urban+agriculture.

108–109 Adapted from *Gestures: the Do's and Taboos of Body Language around the World* by Roger E Axtell. Copyright © John Wiley & Sons, Inc. Reprinted with permission.

112–113 Adapted from "Power napping is good for the IQ", *The Scotsman* 06/06/2000. Reprinted with permission.

115–116 Adapted from "Common questions about dreams". Copyright © 2010. All Rights Reserved, International Association for the Study of Dreams (IASD) http://asdreams.org.

118–119 Adapted from "Can it be a wake-up call?" by Lea Wee, Sunday Plus, *The Straits Times* (Singapore), 05/30/1999. Copyright © Singapore Press Holdings Limited. Reprinted with permission.

Art Credits

Illustration credits: 21 Matt Collins and Steve Schell; 22–23 Matt Collins and Steve Schell; 61 Steve Schell; 66 Don Williams/Page Designs International, Inc; 68–69 Steve Schell.

Photo credits: 1 (t) Stewart Cohen/Stone/Getty Images, (c) ©iStockphoto.com/Thomas_EyeDesign, (b) Gallo Images/Getty Images; 2–3 kaetana - Fotolia.com; 2 Stewart Cohen/Stone/Getty Images; 5 (tl) ©iStockphoto.com/Thomas_EyeDesign, (tr) Juice Images/Getty Images, (c) Pawel Gaul/Getty Images, (bl) Pascal Broze/Getty Images, (br) JGI/Jamie Grill/Getty Images; 8 Gallo Images/Getty Images; 11 (t) ©Supri Suharjoto*, (c) ©Stocklite*, (b) REUTERS/Chip East; 12–13 Elnur - Fotolia.com; 12 Supri Suharjoto*; 15 ©Stocklite*; 18–19 Irochka - Fotolia.com; 18 REUTERS/Chip East; 21 (t) Image Source/Getty Images, (b) Jupiterimages/Getty Images/Thinkstock; 25 Image Source/Getty Images; 28 (tl) Jupiterimages/Thinkstock, (tc) ©Epicstockmedia*, (tr) ©iStockphoto.com/Dvanphoto, (bl) ©Galyna Andrushko*, (bc) Jupiterimages/Getty Images/Thinkstock, (br) Vitalii Nesterchuk*; 31 (t) Roy Mehta/Getty Images, (c) Svenja-Foto/Corbis, (b) Blend Images/SuperStock; 32 Roy Mehta/Getty Images; 33 (l to r) Monkey Business - Fotolia.com, (2) CandyBox Images - Fotolia.com, (3) boumenjapet - Fotolia.com, (4) nyul - Fotolia.com, (5) helix - Fotolia.com; 35 Svenja-Foto/Corbis; 36 Tony Avelar/The Christian Science Monitor/The Image Works; 38–39 PHILETDOM - Fotolia.com; 38 Blend Images/Superstock; 41 (t) Ricardo Moraes/AP Images, (c) David White/Alamy Images, (b) ©iStockphoto/Thinkstock; 42–43 Ricardo Moraes/AP Images; 42 ©Natursports*; 45 David White/Alamy; 48–49 WuTtY - Fotolia.com; 48 ©iStockphoto/Thinkstock; 51 (t) Digital Vision/Thinkstock, (c) ©iStockphoto/Thinkstock, (b) ©iStockphoto.com/sjlocke; 52–53 Digital Vision/Thinkstock; 54 (l to r, t to b) Elnur - Fotolia.com, (2) emily2k - Fotolia.com, (3) Vladimir Voronin - Fotolia.com, (4) Paul Maguire - Fotolia.com, (5) Elenathewise - Fotolia.com, (6) Aaron Kohr - Fotolia.com, (7) Feng Yu - Fotolia.com, (8) angelo.gi - Fotolia.com; 55 ©iStockphoto/Thinkstock; 56 (t) LatitudeStock/Alamy, (b) ©iStockphoto.com/LazingBee; 58–59 Alexander Mitiuc - Fotolia.com; 58 ©iStockphoto.com/sjlocke; 61 (t) Jetta Productions/Getty Images, (b) Purestock/Getty Images; 62–63 Ljupco Smokovski - Fotolia.com; 62 (t) Jetta Productions/Getty Images, (b) ©Omer N Raja*; 65 Purestock/Getty Images; 71 (t) George Doyle/Thinkstock, (c) Comstock/Thinkstock, (b) Tetra Images/Getty Images; 72–73 gunnar3000 - Fotolia.com; 72 George Doyle/Thinkstock; 75 Comstock/Thinkstock; 78–79 yellowj - Fotolia.com; 78 Tetra Images/Getty Images; 81 (t) ©Iofoto*, (c) Nick Clements/Getty Images, (b) ©iStockphoto/Thinkstock; 82 ©iofoto*; 82–83 kmit - Fotolia.com; 85 Nick Clements/Getty Images; 88–89 Roman Milert - Fotolia.com; 88 ©iStockphoto/Thinkstock; 91 (t) Roberto Westbrook/Getty Images, (c) Masterfile Royalty Free, (b) Adamsmith/Getty Images; 92 Roberto Westbrook/Getty Images; 95 Masterfile Royalty Free; 98–99 mashe - Fotolia.com; 98 Adamsmith/Getty Images; 101 (t) ©Ronald Sumners*, (c) Howard Lipin/ZUMA Press/Corbis, (b) Jupiterimages/Thinkstock; 102–103 Mikael Damkier - Fotolia.com; 102 ©Marie C Fields*; 105 Fancy Photography/Sustainable Living/Veer; 109 Jupiterimages/Thinkstock; 111 (t) Pixland/Thinkstock, (c) Ajphoto/Photo Researchers, (b) ©iStockphoto.com/digitalskillet; 112–113 Pixland/Thinkstock; 115 AJPhoto/Photo Researchers, Inc.; 118–119 HaywireMedia - Fotolia.com; 118 ©iStockphoto.com/digitalskillet.

*2011 Used under license from Shutterstock.com